Making Jams and Preserves

By Diana Sutton

The Good Life Press LTD

Published by The Good Life Press Ltd. 2008

ISBN 978 1 90487 135 4
A catalogue record for this book is available from
the British Library.

Published by
The Good Life Press Ltd.
PO Box 536
Preston
PR2 9ZY

www.goodlifepress.co.uk
www.homefarmer.co.uk
www.precycle-it.co.uk

Set by The Good Life Press Ltd.
Printed and bound in Great Britain
by Paper4u Ltd

Making Jams and Preserves

By Diana Sutton

Dedication

This is for Paul, my inspiration for life.

With love.

Contents

Introduction

Throughout history we have depended on preserving food to enable us to survive the winter months. Before canning, freezing and other mechanical methods, drying and salting meats and vegetables and drying fruit were the only methods available to preserve foodstuffs so we became fairly good at it. It was inevitable that some fruit was wasted as gluts meant there was so much ready for picking in a short space of time, and much of the harvest would be used to make drinks.

Because sugar wasn't readily available, nor reasonably priced, jam and marmalade making didn't generally happen until the 17th century, though there is a record of marmalade being made in England in 1587. The first record of jam making was in 1730, though it isn't clear how far back preserving fruit by the making of jams extends. But it has been an invaluable means of preserving fruit and vegetables in the form of chutneys and pickles for the last couple of centuries. It is still true today, especially for those who have home-grown fruit and vegetables in abundance and don't know what to do with it all.

It is also a great pleasure to buy or to be given produce to make your own as there is nothing more satisfying than being able to say, 'I made it myself.' As for flavour, there is no comparison;

even the most expensive jams and preserves do not taste as good as home made.

For many years jams and preserves have been entered into competions at food fairs, Women's Institute shows and Church bazaars.

Making your own preserves isn't necessarily cheaper than purchasing the same unless you do grow your own, but it is still worthwhile for the satisfaction and taste alone. You won't need lots of equipment and tools. It is also certainly easier than most people think and the recipes in this book cover all degrees of difficulty and methods.

When I first started making jam I was amazed at the speed of the process and how little time it takes to get the desired result, so don't be put off by the idea that it is too time consuming. So long as you have everything prepared and ready it will not take long to produce something so delicious you will wonder why you didn't make it before.

Microwave ovens enable us to make preserves in smaller batches in a very short space of time. Marmalade is the best candidate for this as the traditional method can take a long time to cook because of the hard rinds and peels of citrus fruits. They are also useful for pre-cooking the fruit and vegetables to shorten the cooking time on the hob before the other ingredients need to be added.

Making your own jams and preserves is a great way of re-using jars and bottles. So long as they have good lids they will be good enough to use for home preserving. Most of the recipes make average amounts of preserve so you will not end up with jars and jars for which you will have to find storage.

Finally, you will know exactly what has gone into the making your jams, chutneys, preserves and ketchups if you have made them yourself. I have used no preservatives except for the natural preserving qualities of sugar and vinegar. They will not necessarily keep for as long as a commercially made product, but the satisfaction of having made them yourself makes it worthwhile.

Diana Sutton
Manchester
2008

Chapter One
Some Preserving Facts

Preserving your own fruit and vegetables is one of the best ways to use up a glut of produce, either home grown or purchased. Making your own allows a wider range of choice and variations than is available in the shops, and once you have mastered the essentials you can begin to experiment.

Always bear in mind that making your own preserves should not be a way of using up poor quality produce. It is of the utmost importance that only fruit and vegetables at their very peak are used as just a small proportion of poor quality foodstuffs will cause the whole batch to spoil.

Preserving is used to kill off any spoiling bacteria or organisms present on the fruit and vegetables. Washing is not sufficient to do this, though it is the first step to clean and preserve any produce. The act of preservation is done in two ways; firstly, by boiling up the fruit and vegetables and secondly, by poisoning them. This may sound a little extreme, but vinegar messes up the metabolism of bacteria, thus killing them and the sugar causes their downfall by osmotically changing their water content.

Once the spoiling bacteria have been killed off you must make sure it stays that way so that anything airborn that lands on it during the preparation process will also be killed osmotically due to the high sugar content. It just so happens that this process of using vinegar and sugar also enhances the flavours of the foodstuffs used, as during the cooking time the sugar draws out the water from the fruit or vegetables, therefore concentrating their flavour, and the resulting juices also serve to flavour the rest of the materials which make up the preserve. The flavour then is also preserved for months rather than days.

So why do we have to sterilise the lids and jars and seal each one so thoroughly?

The reason for this is that the jar's contents can create a less osmotically strong environment and so spoilage could still occur after a few weeks.

Sealing is also vitally important due again to osmosis, as the solution used to preserve the food draws water from the atmosphere, therefore diluting it and making it more susceptible to contamination. A strong seal is vital for thorough preservation. So a jar of preserves once opened needs to be used up fairly rapidly, though storage in the fridge lengthens its shelf-life somewhat.

The main preservatives used in making jams, marmalades and chutneys are sugar and vinegar and, though you do use salt for flavour, it is not in sufficient quantities to act as a preservative. In jams, conserves, marmalades and jellies it is obviously only sugar that is used. In chutneys and relishes both sugar and vinegar are used, the latter serving to pickle it, with sugar often added solely for taste.

What is the difference between all the different kinds of preserves?

Jam is crushed fruit boiled to a thick consistency and preserved by adding sugar. It doesn't matter what kind of fruit is used.

Marmalades are jams that use any citrus fruit, usually cooked with thinly sliced pieces of peel.

Jellies are the juices of fruit boiled to a thick consistency and preserved by the addition of sugar.

Conserves are jams made with whole fruit and often have the addition of dried fruit, nuts or some form of alcohol.

Fruit curds are pulped fruits cooked with eggs and sugar, but will only keep for about four weeks in the fridge or two in a cool dark cupboard.

Cheeses and butters are stewed fruits made into a pulp, to which sugar is added, but they are not boiled together. Cheese has equal weights of both fruit pulp and sugar and butters have half the weight of sugar to fruit. See the individual recipes for more information.

Pickles are fruit or vegetables preserved in vinegar, usually with added spices. The aim is to preserve the shape and colour of the produce as far as possible, though there may be some alteration in colour.

Chutneys have all kinds of things in them, often combining fruits, vegetables, herbs and spices. You will also find dried fruits used alongside fresh, and vinegar and sugar used as the preservatives.

Before the British colonised the subcontinent, the idea of cooking in vinegar was not known in the UK, but was very widely used in the Far East.

In Georgian times, when the growing of tomatoes, or love apples as they were known, became popular on a wide scale in the glasshouses of major estates, the first green tomato chutneys were devised. A greenhouse full of green tomatoes is a pretty dismal sight, and a good boiling in sweet vinegar made the piquant sauce that gentlemen returning from India so admired.

Chutneys are cooked almost to a pulp texture with perhaps just a little bite to them. It comes down to a matter of taste and which produce you are using to make the chutney.

Some Preserving Facts

Relishes are now synonomously linked with both burgers and kebabs and are an ideal accompaniment due to the fresh flavours contained in them. They can be either cooked or raw, but the raw version obviously cannot be classed as a preserve.The cooked variety may be kept for a longer period of time, though not as long as a chutney as they are not boiled for as long.

Check each recipe for the length of storage life of each type of preserve. Though most are best refrigerated once opened, the high sugar content of some recipes means that they may be stored in a cupboard and kept for a few weeks if needed.

The real success of making preserves is remembering a few vital steps, most intended to keep out anything that may spoil the finished product. Using top quality produce, washing thoroughly, having clean, sterilised utensils and equipment and, as each recipe is different due to the properties of the fruit or vegetables used, it is important to follow closely the instructions in the recipe. So enjoy making your own preserves and be proud of your hard work. ❧

Chapter Two
Getting Started

Equipment

Jam and preserve making needs very little in the way of specialist utensils. Jams and marmalades can be made in an ordinary sturdy pan. Be sure the pan is large enough to hold at least double the quantity of jam you wish to make and has a strong handle. If you wish to regularly make lots of preserves it is going to be worthwhile buying the correct equipment that will survive extensive use. The pan you use makes all the difference to how confident you feel about making preserves so, if you buy nothing else for your preserve making, buy a preserving pan. You can also use the same pan to make fudges, caramels and toffees.

Preserving pans are made so that the heat is evenly distibuted throughout the contents of the pan, so you don't get hot spots that may cause burning or over cooking of the fruit. They are usually made from aluminium or stainless steel, but aluminium can taint the fruits and vegetables with an acidic content, so it is best to stick with a stainless steel pan. Copper pans are also not suitable, as once again the metal reacts with the acid content of the ingredients and taints the finished product.

Making Jams and Preserves

A preserving, or a maslin pan as they are known, can be purchased from most good kitchen stores and online. It needs to be a wide pan to allow the speedy evaporation of water from the ingredients. Choose the best you can afford and make sure it holds at least 9 litres, has a pouring lip and a handle for ease of movement and safety.

The other four products essential for the easy making of preserves are a long handled jam spoon, a wide-necked preserving funnel, a thermometer and a reliable set of scales.

A preserving spoon has a longer handle than a normal wooden spoon and usually a flat edge that can reach all the areas of the base of your pan to make stiring both easier and more thorough.

A wide-necked preserving funnel is a must to enable you to ladle or pour your preserves into the jars. You will thus have no worries about trying to aim your jam through the narrow tops of the jars and therefore no spillage. This funnel can also be used for transferring dry ingredients from packets to other containers with ease. A tip - buy a cheap, ordinary plastic funnel and cut round the base of the 'bowl.'

The preserving thermometer is another bit of equipment that makes preparation easier. They come with easy to use descriptions of what each temperature does to the sugar and inform you when the setting point has been reached. You don't have to keep testing for the setting point, although it's a good idea when first starting to make jams and preserves to check manually so that you know what to look for and the approximate timings for the various recipes.

The thermometer is cased in stainless steel and should show both degrees farenheit and celsius. It can also be used for making fudges and toffees as it will tell you when the various stages of texture have been achieved; either soft or hard ball, soft or hard crack etc. A good thermometer has a movable clip on the back to enable you to rest it safely on the side of the pan, giving you both hands free to cook the preserve. Before use always dip the thermometer in warm water before immersing it in the hot preserve.

Even though your pan has a pouring lip, a ladle with a lip is an excellent utensil to use when filling your jars, especially with thick chutneys and relishes. You will also have more control over the amounts and when to stop filling to avoid any spillages.

A set of accurate kitchen scales is required as precise amounts of fruit, vegetables and sugar are often the key to the success of your preserve.
When making jelly preserves you will also need a strainer. A jam strainer or sieve is usually made from nylon, strong muslin or plastic and has a

stand so it may be placed over a bowl to allow the juices to flow freely from the fruit.

A heat-proof jug to measure the amounts of juice and liquids is also essential, especially in jelly-making.

Other spoons, bowls and containers may be needed for the different recipes. Some chutney and pickle recipes have very precise amounts of spices in them, so having a set of measuring spoons is also useful. A perforated spoon is also useful for taking off any scum or floating seeds that you need to get rid of.

Have some muslin bags or squares ready to hold the pips and any discarded pith in the recipes, as the pips and pith both contain a high percentage of pectin that will help the preserves to set well.

Jars, labels and covers

You can purchase jars specially for preserving and bottling, but re-using jam and marmalade jars which have secure lids is ideal. Always make sure they will withstand high temperatures as the preserves are extremely hot when poured into the jars as this is part of the long term preserving process. It is good to also have a few special jars set aside for when you want to present the preserves as gifts, and kilner jars are useful for chutneys and pickles. For lids it is best to use the most secure way to seal your jams and preserves. I have found that a screw type is the best way to keep the jam from spoiling, but you can also buy waxed discs and cloth covers that are secured with string rather than rubber bands, as they can slacken and cause the preserve to spoil.

Labelling is a very important part of preserving, so that you know when all the different preserves were made. You can buy ready made printed labels for you to write on, or you can try printing your own designs on your computer if you have one.

A checklist of basic preserving equipment:

Preserving pan
Long handled spoon
Wide-necked funnel
Jam thermometer
Kitchen scales
Jelly sieve or straining bag
A heat-proof jug
A ladle
A perforated spoon
Small measuring spoons
Bowls and basins
Jars, labels and covers

The importance of sterilizing jars and utensils.

As with all food preparation, cleanliness is an absolute must, but when preserving food in any way, all preserving jars, bottles and lids must be sterile. It only takes a small amount of contamination to spoil a whole jar of preserves. There are several ways to sterilize your jars and containers.

Wash your jars thoroughly in hot soapy water and rinse well prior to all methods.

Then either:

Place the jars on a baking tray and put in a preheated oven at 120°C/Gas ½ for 20 minutes.

Place the jars in boiling water in a large pan and turn down the heat to a simmer for 5 minutes. Metal or heat resistant plastic lids can also be prepared in this way.

Microwave each jar containing a little boiled water for 1 full minute.

Use a Milton type solution as you would for babies' feeding equipment, simply following the instructions on the back of the pack. For the most part lids are best sterilized in this way.

Chapter Three
Basic Jam Making

The following stages of preparation and cooking are intended solely for jam and each individual recipe may have its own steps to follow. The steps below give reasons why each stage is important and why it is done. For many basic jams this would be all you need to know, except for quantities. In the jam recipes that follow you will find quantities and also a quick resumé of the method needed for simple jams. More complex jams will all provide fully explained methods.

Step 1 - Preparing the fruit

Chose fruit that is as fresh as possible. Firm, just ripe fruit is the best, but small amounts of slightly under-ripe fruit may also be used. Over-ripe fruit isn't as good for two reasons. Firstly, over-ripe fruit may contain bacteria and moulds that could spoil the flavour of the batch of jam and, although they would be detroyed in the cooking process, it isn't worth risking tainting the whole panful. Secondly, fruit loses its pectin content as it over-ripens, so the setting of the jam becomes more difficult.

The fruit must be washed thoroughly and hull strawberries, raspberries and any other soft fruit. Top and tail gooseberries, currants and elderberries. Peel and core apples and pears and stoned fruit such as plums and apricots. Cherries and damsons may be cooked with the stones in, but I would sooner have the work of de-stoning done before I have to eat the jam, as messing about with them afterwards spoils my enjoyment. Remember, when picking fruit from the wild always do it when the fruit is as dry as possible, preferably when the sun is out and any dew on the fruit has had time to dry off.

Step 2 - Cooking the Fruit

After washing and preparing the fruit, place it in your pan to pre-cook. This softens the fruit and gets the juices running and the pectin flowing. Sometimes a small amount of water may be needed, depending on the fruit. Details of this are included in each individual recipe as necessary.

Bring the fruit slowly to the boil, then simmer until it is tender. Try not to stir the fruit too much as this tends to break it too soon and you will therefore lose some of the flavour of the finished product. If you have a deep layer of fruit some gentle stirring will be necessary though, to allow all the fruit to cook evenly. The acid content of the fruit is also released in this first cooking time and this helps the pectin to set the jam. If you are using fruits low in acid this would be the stage at which you would add acid, usually in the form of lemon juice. Again, each individual recipe will include this as required according to the fruit used.

Fruits with low acid content include strawberries, raspberries, late picked blackberries, cherries, dessert apples, bilberries, peaches, pears and quinces.

Step 3 - All about Pectin

Pectin is the setting or gelling agent found naturally in varying degrees in fruit and vegetables. Without pectin jams and preserves would never set sufficiently. It is found in the cell walls and is broken down by heating.

The pectin reacts with the sugar to gel the juices and set. It requires the presence of acid to gel properly. If a fruit is naturally low in pectin you can add some. This is either through a home-made pectin stock or by buying a sachet of dried pectin. Specialist sugars may also contain additional pectin.

Some fruit has a medium pectin content and so may require just a small addition. Fruits high in pectin will not need any adding. These fruits are often good to team up with fruits with a low pectin content.

Making Jams and Preserves

Fruit High Pectin Content	Fruit with Medium Pectin Content	Fruit with Low Pectin Content
Cooking apples	Early picked blackberries	Late picked blackberries
Red Currents	Apricots	Dessert Apples
Blackcurrants	Greengages	Strawberries
Gooseberries	Loganberries	Bilberries
Damsons	Rhubarb	Quinces
Cranberries	Raspberries	Cherries
Plums		Peaches
		Pears

If necessary pectin is added before the addition of sugar, after cooking the fruit.

Commercially produced pectin is usually sold in powdered form in single sachets. It is essential that you follow the manufacturers instructions for the amounts used. Each sachet of the make I use is designed for use with 1kg of sugar.

Sugar that already contains pectin is useful for very low pectin content fruits.

Recipe for Pectin Stock

This is prepared from either cooking apples, gooseberries or red currants as all these fruits have the highest available pectin content.

1kg / 2.2lbs cooking apples, gooseberries
or red currants
435ml / ¾ pint water

Place the fruit and water in a pan and bring to the boil. Reduce the heat and simmer until tender.

Strain the juices using a jelly strainer and set them aside in a clean jug. Put the pulp back in the pan and allow it to cool completely. After cooling, allow it to stand for an hour and then add half the original amount of water. Bring it to simmering point and cook slowly for 1 hour. Strain as before and combine the two yields of juice. Bring both the juices to the boil and cook at boiling for 5 minutes.

Place it in sterilised bottles with secure lids.

To use.

Approximately 250ml / 8fl oz pectin stock per 1kg / 2.2lb of fruit low in pectin or 125ml / 4oz pectin stock per 1kg / 2.2lb of fruit with a medium pectin content.

Step 4 - Adding the Sugar

Any type of white sugar may be used to make jams and preserves. Brown sugar alters the flavour of the jam and gives it a caramel flavour that can spoil the full fruit flavour required. Granulated, caster, lump or preserving sugar can all be used successfully. Preserving sugar has the added benefit of producing very little scum during cooking, but a small knob of butter does the same job with ordinary granulated sugar. It also dissolves slightly quicker, but again this isn't a problem as the difference is very small. It is much more expensive than ordinary granulated too, so have a go with it if you wish and see which one you prefer.

There are some things to remember when adding your amounts of sugar. Use too little sugar and the jam will not set properly, though some preserves are good if slightly runny. Use too much and the flavour will be impaired, so always stick to the amount of sugar stated in the recipe as this is usually correct for the best setting and the best flavour of the finished jam. Sugar also helps to preserve the jam and if you use less sugar you will shorten its storage life. There are some recipes in this book that do use less sugar. Where appropriate a shelf life is given for them, both un-opened and opened.

Before the sugar is added, make sure that your

sugar is either at room temperature or if not then warm it in a low oven in an ovenproof dish for 10 minutes. This is to stop the fruit from cooling too much as the sugar is added. Keep the pan on a low heat while adding the sugar as one of the most important things to do next is to thoroughly dissolve it prior to boiling. If you don't do this you will produce a grainy jam that does not keep and will have wasted your fruit and sugar. Stir the jam gently as the sugar dissolves as this will speed up the process. Test that it has all dissolved by allowing the jam to run down the back of the spoon and if the grains of sugar have gone then it is ready to be boiled. Continue heating slowly and stirring if the jam still looks grainy.

Step 5- Boiling the Jam

Bring to the boil as quickly as you can, still stirring gently. If scum rises to the surface then add a knob of butter and this will get rid of it. Keep the jam boiling rapidly for at least 4 minutes, then begin testing for a set. Do not over boil it as this will stop the jam from setting or will harden the sugar and make it unusable. Better a soft set which can still be used as it is very palatable! Using a thermometer makes recognising the setting point much easier as it is the temperature the sugar reaches that determines the setting point. The temperature of the setting point is 105°C / 220°F. It is also good to use one of the other tests too, just to be sure. There are two manual ways to check for setting,

1.The saucer test - using a very cold saucer, drop a little of the jam on to it. The jam should cool almost immediately. If the setting point has been reached a skin will form on the surface and when pushed with a finger it will wrinkle and remain wrinkled.

2.The flake method - spoon up a little jam and allow it to cool. Turn the spoon on its side and allow the jam to run down. If it runs together and falls down in large flakes it is ready. If it runs in thin streams and little flakes it needs extra boiling time.

I find the saucer test the quickest method as the jam cools quickly on the cool saucer and it is easier to actually see the setting point. Some jams will naturally produce a soft set which means they will not be as thick in texture and will not hold their shape as well as a firm set jam. But these jams have the advantage of having a wonderful fruity flavour and are often associated with jams made with whole fruit, especially the ones with a low pectin content. Don't add more pectin than stated in a recipe as this will spoil the flavour of the jam, giving it a bitter aftertaste.

Step 6 - Removing the Scum

When the setting point is reached, if there is any

scum on the top of the jam, either add a knob of butter and stir in gently or use a straining spoon to remove the top layer of scum. As the boiling subsides so will the bubbles of air that caused the scum to appear.

Step 7- Bottling and Sealing the Jam

Fill the jars whilst the jam is very hot. Just off the boil is best as this helps with the preservation of the jam. This can affect the distribution of whole fruit pieces in the jam. If you have kept some of the fruit whole during cooking, this will need to be distributed evenly throughout the jam. It is therefore best to allow the jam to cool for about 20 minutes or until a skin begins to form on the top. Cover the pan during this process to stop anything contaminating the jam. The jars you use must be sterilised. See chapter 2 for ways of doing this. To help you fill your jars use a funnel and a ladle. This will give you more control over the amounts. The jars must be filled right to the top and wipe away any drips on the sides of the jars. Cover the surface with a waxed disc before placing on the lid or securing the cover.

Step 8 - Labelling the Jars

This is a very important stage in the storage of your jam, especially if you make large batches. Having a little book where you write down the dates and details, including the recipe used for each batch of jam, will help if you get any problems with it. You will then be able to identitfy any other jars from that batch and check them for any spoilage.

Step 9 - Storing your Jam

Correct storage is essential if you want your jam to keep for its optimum length of time. A cool, dark cupboard or pantry is ideal. If you have an outside store don't allow the jam to freeze or the jars may crack and spoil the contents.

Using Preserved Fruit in Making Jam

You can make jam using most methods of preserving fruit. It lengthens the storage time and is great if you have a large harvest of fruit. Home-frozen fruit can be made into jam as can bottled fruit too. The pectin content will have diminished, however, so setting may be a problem and it isn't good to add too much pectin as it alters the flavour of the jam. Some dried fruits are very good for jam-making and are often used in recipes to both enhance and vary jam flavours. ❧

Apricot Jam

This is a very versatile jam because of its delicate flavour.

Makes approximately 3kg / 6lb

2kg / 4lb fresh apricots
2kg / 4lb sugar
240ml / 9fl oz water

1. Halve and stone the fruit and remove 8-9 kernels from the stones. Blanch them in boiling water and reserve them for cooking with the jam. If you prefer smaller pieces of fruit, quarter the apricots before cooking.

2. Place the apricots, water and kernels in the pan and simmer for 25-30 minutes until the fruit is tender. Remove the kernels.

3. Add the sugar and continue simmering until it has dissolved, stirring gently and constantly.

4. Bring to the boil and cook for 8-10 minutes. Test for the setting point.

5. Cool for a few minutes before potting.

This should keep for up to a year unopened.

Bilberry Jam

This is a rich, dark purple jam that goes really well with scones and cream. The fruit is very tart and requires plenty of sugar but this also helps with the setting of the jam.

1.5kg / 3lb bilberries, topped and tailed
2kg / 4lb sugar
2 x 13g sachets pectin or
190ml / 7fl oz pectin stock
Juice of 1 lemon

1. Place the prepared fruit in the pan with the lemon juice and simmer for 5 minutes.

2. Add the sugar and pectin and stir until it is completely dissolved.

3. When all the sugar is dissolved bring it to the boil and cook at boiling for 4 minutes.

4. Check for the setting point and, when ready, stir and pot the jam.

This should keep for up to a year unopened.

Blackberry Jam

Blackberries herald the beginning of the season. They are a very accessible fruit for harvesting from the wild, so if you are lucky enough to know a good place to go picking blackberries, take the family and enjoy some food for free.

Makes approximately 5kg / 10lb

3kg / 6lb blackberries
3kg / 6lb sugar
150ml / 5fl oz water
Juice of 2 lemons
3 x 13g sachets or
280ml / ½ pint pectin stock

1. Place the fruit in a pan with the water and lemon juice. Heat to simmering and cook for about 5-6 minutes until the fruit is tender.

2. Add the sugar and pectin and continue to cook slowly stirring gently until all the sugar has dissolved.

3. Bring to the boil and and cook rapidly for 8-10 minutes until setting point is reached.

4. Remove any scum and pot immediately.

This should keep for 8-9 months unopened.

Blackberry and Apple Jam

2kg / 4lb blackberries, hulled
1kg / 2lb Bramley apples, peeled, cored
and thinly sliced
Juice of 1 lemon
3kg / 6lb sugar
280ml / ½ pint water

1. Simmer the apples and half of the water for 10 minutes.

2. Add the blackberries and the lemon juice and the rest of the water. Simmer for an extra 10 minutes until the apples are pulpy and the blackberries tender.

3. Add the sugar and stir until completely dissolved.

4. Boil rapidly to the setting point and pot.

This should keep for up to a year unopened.

Blackcurrant Jam

This fruit also gives a high yield of jam per kilo of fruit.

Makes approximately 4kg / 8lb

2kg / 4lb blackcurrants
3kg / 6lb sugar
1.2 litres / 2pints water

1. Place the prepared blackcurrants in a pan with the water and bring to the boil. Reduce the heat and simmer for 30 minures until the fruit is tender. Stir occasionally as the mixture thickens.

2. Whilst the blackcurrants are cooking, heat the sugar in a low oven for 10 minutes.

3. Remove the pan from the heat and stir in the sugar. Allow it to dissolve fully on a low heat.

4. When the sugar has fully dissolved turn up the heat and bring to the boil.

5. Boil for 5 minutes then check for setting point. When the setting point is reached skim off any scum and ladle into pots.

This should keep for up to 1 year unopened.

Bramley Apple Jam

The apples don't need to be peeled, but if you don't want it in your finished jam then peel them and put it in a muslin bag with the cores.

Makes 5kg / 10lb

3kg / 6lb Bramley apples
3kg / 6lb sugar
4 tablespoons lemon juice
1 litre / 2 pints water
1 level teaspoon cinnamon (optional)

1. Halve and core the unpeeled apples. Slice and dice them very thinly and put them in the water and lemon juice. Put the cores in a muslin bag.

2. Put the prepared apples, the water they were in and the muslin bag with the cores in the pan.

3. Simmer until the apples begin to pulp. Add the sugar (and cinnamon if you are using it) and dissolve, stirring gently.

4. Boil rapidly and test for the setting point after 5 minutes.

5. Allow the jam to cool a little, then ladle it into jars.

This should keep for up to a year unopened.

Cherry Jam

Cherries are low in pectin and acid, but both can be added.

Makes approximately 2kg / 4lb

1.5kg / 3lb cherries
1kg / 2lb sugar
Juice of 2 lemons
1 x 13g sachet of pectin

1. Stone the cherries and tie about 12 of them up in a muslin bag.

2. Place the cherries, lemon juice and the 12 stones in a pan and simmer for 30 minutes.

3. Take out the bag of stones, add the pectin and stir in the sugar.

4. Dissolve the sugar slowly, stirring well but gently so as not to mash up all the cherries.

5. When the sugar has dissolved fully, boil rapidly for 4 minutes and test for setting.

6. Allow to cool for 5 minutes before stirring carefully and ladling into pots.

This should keep for 4-5 months in a cool dark place unopened.

Damson Jam

This dark, tangy jam has a wonderful flavour and the fruit contains a high pectin content. Damsons also give a good yield of jam per kilo of fruit. Some prefer to cook the fruit before stoning but I find I miss many of the stones and don't like the idea of one in my finished jam. I tend to do it before, catching and saving bits of juice as I do so to add to the jam. It is tricky though.

Makes approximately 4.5kg / 9lb

2.5kg / 5lb damsons
3kg / 6lb sugar
850ml / 1½ pints water

1. Place the fruit and water in the pan and simmer for 20 minutes until the damsons are tender. This may take less time if you have already stoned the fruit.

2. Add the sugar and stir gently until it has dissolved completely.

3. Bring to the boil and test for setting after about 10 minutes of boiling or when your thermometer indicates.

4. Stir and pot immediately.

This should keep for up to a year unopened.

Dried Apricot Jam

This recipe contains flaked almonds. These may be omitted, if preferred. It has a much richer flavour than jam made with fresh apricots.

Makes approximately 4.5 kg / 8-9lb

1kg / 2lb dried apricots
Juice of 2 lemons
3kg / 6lb sugar
75g / 2oz flaked almonds

1. Soak the dried apricots in water for at least 24 hours. Place the soaked apricots and the liquid into a pan with the lemon juice.

2. Bring to the boil, then reduce the heat and simmer the fruit for 30 minutes, stirring occasionally.

3. Add the almonds and remove from the heat whilst adding the sugar. Return to a low heat and stir until all the sugar has dissolved.

4. Turn up the heat and bring to the boil, cooking at a rapid boil for 5-6 minutes. Then test.

5. Pot immediately when ready.

This should keep for more than a year unopened.

Elderberry Jam

2kg / 4lb elderberries
2.8kg / 5½lb sugar
1.8litres / 3 pints water

1. Remove the berries from their stalks with a fork and place them in the pan with the water.

2. Bring to the boil, crushing the fruit to release the juice. Cook at a light boil for 10 minutes.

3. Stir in the sugar and continue stirring until it has all dissolved.

4. Bring back to the boil and continue for about 10-15 minutes until the setting point is reached.

5. Pot immediately in sterilized jars.

This should keep for 10-12 months unopened.

Gooseberry Jam

Use gooseberries that are not quite ripe for this recipe. Don't worry if there are some ripe ones amongst them so long as the majority of the fruit is under-ripe. This will mean that the fruit contains its optimum level of pectin, so a good set is guarenteed.

Makes about 4.5kg / 8lb

2.2kg / 4lb 8oz gooseberries
3kg / 6lb sugar
850ml / 1½ pints water

1. Top and tail the gooseberries and put them in a pan with the water. Simmer for 20 minutes or until the skins pop and they begin to pulp.

2. Add the sugar and stir until it has dissolved.

3. Turn up the heat and boil rapidly for 10 minutes, then test for setting.

4. Allow it to cool for a few seconds before putting it into jars.

This should keep for up to 1 year unopened.

Gooseberry and Elderflower Jam

This is a very refeshing summery preserve and tastes wonderful with a slice of Madeira cake or some freshly baked bread. If you only want a hint of elderflower then use only 2 heads of the plant, but use a greater quantity for a stronger flavour.

Makes approximately 4.5 kg / 9lb

2kg / 4lb gooseberries, topped and tailed
720ml / 1¼ pints of water
2.5kg / 5lb sugar
2-5 elderflower heads, washed

1. Place the elderflower heads in a muslin bag and secure. Place this in the pan with the gooseberries and water and simmer until the fruit is tender. Bring to the boil for 2 minutes. Remove the heads and squeeze any juice from the bag into the fruit.

2. Add the sugar and stir until dissolved.

3. Boil for 10 minutes, then test for the setting point.

4. Stir and pour into pots.

This should keep for up to a year unopened.

Greengage Jam

Greengages can be quite dry so a little extra water may be needed. Check on the texture when halving and stoning the gages. If they look dry add a further 240ml / 8fl oz of water when cooking the fruit.

Makes 5kg / 10lb

3kg / 6lb greengages, halved and stoned,
3kg / 6lb sugar
560ml / 1 pint water (or more)
12 kernels, removed from the stone and blanched in boiling water

1. Place the prepared fruit in the pan with the water and kernels and simmer until the gages are soft, stirring occasionally.

2. When the fruit is soft bring it to the boil and maintain this for 4 minutes, stirring constantly. Test for setting and continue to boil for another minute if not ready, then test again.

3. When the setting point is reached, allow it to cool for 10 minutes to permit the fruit to settle. Stir it gently and pour into jars.

This jam should keep for up to months unopened.

Hedgerow Jam

Makes about 3kg/6lb

250g / 8oz rosehips
500g / 1lb blackberries
500g / 1lb elderberries
500g / 1lb crab apples
250g / 8oz sloes
250g / 8oz rowan berries
1.5kg / 3lb sugar

1. Wash all the fruit thoroughly.

2. Chop up the crab apples and put them into the pan with the rosehips, rowan berries and sloes.

3. Pour over just enough water to cover the fruit and cook until tender.

4. Sieve the pulp, making sure you get as much as possible through the sieve.

5. Return it to the pan with the blackberries and elderberries and simmer for 15 minutes.

6. Add the sugar and stir until dissolved.

7. Boil rapidly for 10 minutes, then test for the setting point. When ready, pot and seal.

This should keep for 3-4 months unopened.

High Dumpsy Dearie Jam

I have no idea why this jam is so called. It originates from Worcestershire, so if anyone can enlighten me, please do so. I do know it is an excellent jam to use up all of the autumnal fruits left over from the harvest. If you have more pears than plums or more apples than plums then don't worry, so long as the overall weight of the fruit is about 3kg / 6lb. This makes a wonderful base for a steamed sponge pudding.

Makes approximately 3.5kg / 7lb

1kg / 2lb Bramley or other cooking apples, peeled, cored and sliced
1kg / 2lb pears, peeled, cored and sliced
1kg / 2lb plums, halved and stoned
2kg / 4lb 8oz sugar
The rind and juice of 1 lemon
25g / 1oz piece of root ginger
140ml / 5fl oz water

1. Put the rind and the ginger in a muslin bag.

2. Put all the prepared fruit in a pan with the water. A little more water may be needed towards the end of the cooking time. Simmer until tender. This will take about 30-35 minutes. Check the water content and add a little more if the mixture looks dry.

Making Jams and Preserves

3. Add the muslin bag and the lemon juice and cook for 5 more minutes.

4. Stir in the sugar and continue to stir until all the sugar has dissolved.

5. Bring to the boil and cook at boiling for 10 minutes. Remove the muslin bag carefully with tongs.

6. Test for setting. It will not be as firm a set as the apple jam unless you boil it for another 10 minutes, however, the flavour will diminish if you over boil the jam. If you wish for a firmer set, add a 13g sachet of pectin with the sugar and test for setting after just 5 minutes.

7. When the setting point is reached, pot the jam straight away.

This should keep for 5-6 months unopened.

Papaya Jam

1 large, ripe papaya
Juice of 1 lemon
900g / 1lb sugar

1. Peel, de-seed and slice the papaya thinly. Put it into a container and add the lemon juice and sugar. Mix well.

2. Cover and leave it overnight.

3. Purée it in a food processor.

4. Transfer it to a pan, bring to the boil and then reduce to a simmer. Continue cooking until all the moisture has evaporated.

5. Spoon it into jars and store in a cool, dark cupboard.

This will keep for 8-9 months unopened.

Peach and Pear Jam

Both fruits have medium to low pectin content and low acidity so add pectin and lemon juice .

Makes approximately 3.5kg / 7lb

1kg / 2lb peaches
1kg / 2lb pears
2kg /4lb sugar
Juice of 3 lemons
2 x 13g sachets of pectin or
250ml / 9floz stock
120ml / 5fl oz water

1. Peel, stone and core both fruits and chop roughly. Place them in the pan with the water and simmer until just tender.

2. Add the lemon juice and stir in the sugar.

4. When sugar has dissolved, stir in the pectin and bring to the boil.

5. Boil briskly for 4 minutes, then test for the setting point. Continue until the setting point is reached, but don't over boil as the jam will certainly lose some of its flavour.

6. Stir and pot straight away.

This should keep for 5-6 months unopened.

Plum Jam

Use fresh plums if possible. They are higher in pectin.

Makes approximately 5kg / 10lb

3kg / 6lb Victoria plums
3kg / 6lb sugar
560ml / 1 pint water

1. Halve and stone the fruit. If you like smaller pieces of fruit in your jam quarter the plums.

2. Place the fruit in the pan with the water (and the kernels if you are using them) and simmer for the length of time it takes to reduce the liquid by half.

3. Add the sugar and stir until it has dissolved.

4. Bring to the boil and cook at boiling for 6-8 minutes. Remove from the heat and test for setting.

5. Allow to cool for 5 minutes before stirring and potting.

This should store well and should keep for 10-12 months unopened.

Quince Jam

This is a very hard fruit and looks a little like a wrinkly pear that is ready for picking in the autumn. It makes both excellent jam and jelly to serve with roasted game meat. Quince has a honeyed flavour, but requires a lot of sweetening.

Makes approximately 4.5kg / 9lb

2kg / 4lb quinces, peeled, cored & diced
3kg / 6lb sugar
1.5 litres / 3 pints water
Juice of 2 lemons

1. Place the fruit and water in a pan and simmer for at least an hour. Cover it with a lid so that the water doesn't evaporate too quickly.

2. Remove the lid and check to see if the fruit is tender. When it is ready, stir in the sugar and lemon juice and dissolve completely.

3. Continue to simmer together until the liquid begins to thicken slightly, then bring it to the boil until the setting point is reached.

4. Stir and allow it to cool for a few minutes before potting.

This should keep for up to a year unopened.

Raspberry Jam

A basic jam recipe that doesn't need water or pectin.

This quantity makes 3kg / 6lb

2kg / 4lb raspberries
2kg / 4lb sugar
Juice of 1 lemon

1. Place the fruit in your pan and simmer gently for about 10 minutes until the fruit is soft and the juice is running.

2. Remove from the heat and add the lemon juice.

3. Stir in the sugar and place on a low heat. Stir gently but constantly until the sugar is completely dissolved.

4. Turn up the heat and bring to the boil. Cook at boiling for 4 minutes, checking for setting after this time.

5. When the setting point is reached, remove from the heat, cool for 2 or 3 minutes, stir to distribute the fruit evenly and pour into pots and seal.

This should keep for up to 9 months unopened.

Rhubarb Jam

Rhubarb is very low in pectin so use a preserving sugar. This recipe contains root ginger as it goes so well with rhubarb, but if you are not keen then just omit it.

Makes approximately 2.5kg / 5lb

1.5kg / 3lb rhubarb, trimmed and cut
into small chunks
1.5kg / 3lb preserving sugar
Juice of 3 lemons
25g / 1oz root ginger, finely chopped

1. Place all the ingredients in the pan on a low heat and stir until the sugar has dissolved.

2. Continue simmering the mixture until the rhubarb is tender. If they are young stems it should take about 30 minutes, but older rhubarb could take up to 1½ hours.

3. When tender, bring to the boil and cook at boiling for 5-6 minutes until the setting point is reached.

4. Pot immediately and seal.

This should keep for up to 9 months unopened.

Rosehip Jam

500g / 1lb prepared rose hips
1 cup of water
500g / 1lb Sugar

1. Remove the black heads and stems from the hips.

2. Place the rosehips and water together in a large pan.

3. Bring it to the boil, cover and simmer for about 20 minutes until very soft, adding more water if necessary.

4. Press or strain the mixture through a sieve to remove any seeds and to reduce larger chunks of hips.

5. Add the sugar to the pulp and simmer till it is dissolved. Check the taste and add more sugar if desired.

6. Cook until the mixture has thickened to a jam-like consistency.

7. Pour it into sterilized jars and seal well.

This should keep for up to 8-9 months unopened.

Rose Petal Jam

I know it's not very realistic but it does make for a very unusual and pleasant jam, as well as a gift with a real difference. For best effect you should choose deep red and heavily scented roses.

250g / ½lb heavily-scented rose heads
450g / 1lb sugar
2.2 litres / 4 pints water
Juice of 4 lemons

1. Place the petals in a bowl and add half the sugar. Mix to combine them and then cover and leave in a cool place overnight.

2. Add the water, lemon juice and the remaining sugar to a large pan. Heat gently until the sugar has dissolved then stir in the rose petals and sugar prepared previously. Bring to a gentle simmer and cook for 20 minutes.

3. Turn up the heat, bring to the boil and cook for 5 minutes or until the mixture becomes thick. Test for setting.

This should keep for up to 12 months unopened.

Strawberry Jam # 1

This recipe gives a firmer set than the whole fruit one.

Makes approximately 3kg / 6lb

2kg / 4lb strawberries
2kg / 4lb sugar
2 x 13g sachets pectin or
250ml / 8fl oz pectin stock
Juice of 1 lemon

1. Place the prepared fruit in a pan and heat slowly. Crush the fruit with a masher and add the lemon juice.

2. Heat to simmering and cook for 3-4 minutes until the juices run freely.

3. Lower the heat slightly and add the sugar and pectin, stirring until all the sugar has dissolved.

4. Bring to a rapid boil and cook as such for 4-5 minutes. Test for the setting point and, when ready, ladle into jars.

This should keep for up to a year unopened.

Strawberry Jam # 1

Makes approximately 3kg / 6lb

2kg / 4lb strawberries
2kg / 4lb sugar
2 x 13g sachets pectin or
250ml / 8fl oz pectin stock
Juice of 1 lemon

1. Heat the prepared strawberries and sugar together in a pan on a low heat. Try not to stir too much but only to keep the mixture moving or you will break up the fruit.

2. Add the lemon juice. The sugar will gradually dissolve and the juices of the fruit should start to run.

3. When the sugar is fully dissolved add the pectin and bring it quickly to the boil.

4. Test for setting after 4 minutes of continuous boiling. It should have reached its optimum setting point, but remember that it won't be a firm set.

5. Remove it from the heat and stir gently. Pot immediately.

This should store for 6-8 months unopened.

Tropical Fruit Jam

This is fun to make and is a real treat in the centre of a sandwich cake or on top with a little extra coconut. The pieces of pineapple and mango need to be a similar size and the kiwi may be sliced.

Makes approximately 4kg/8lb

2kg / 4lb kiwi fruit
500g / 1lb fresh mango, peeled, stoned and chopped
500g / 1lb fresh pineapple
25g / 1oz dessicated coconut
Juice of 1 lemon
3kg / 6lb sugar
2 x 13g sachets pectin
100ml / 4fl oz water

1. Place all the fruit in the pan with the water and simmer for 5 minutes.

2. Add the lemon juice and stir in the sugar and pectin until the sugar has all dissolved.

3. Add the coconut and bring to the boil. Boil for 4 minutes and test for setting. If it is ready pot it immediately but if not boil for a few more minutes and test again.

This should keep for 8-9 months unopened.

Wild Plum Jam

900g / 2lb of barely ripe wild plums
900g / 2lb of preserving sugar

1. Wash the plums and discard any damaged fruit. Slit them with a knife. This will allow the stones to float to the surface during cooking so that they can easily be removed.

2. Place the prepared plums in a non-metallic bowl, sprinkle over sugar and mix to coat the plums. Cover with a clean tea cloth and leave overnight.

3. The following day put the plums and sugar into a large, heavy bottomed saucepan (or preserving pan) and heat very gently until all the sugar has dissolved.

4. Bring the jam to the boil and continue to boil very rapidly for about 8-10 minutes until the jam reaches the setting point. At this stage carefully remove the stones with a slotted spoon as they float up to the surface.

5. Pour it carefully into sterilised jars,

Store it in a cool, dark place and away from damp.

This will last for 8-9 months unopened.

What have I done wrong?

My jam has got bubbles in it and tastes fizzy.

Reason: The jam is beginning to ferment due to the natural yeasts found in most fruit. This is because there is insufficient sugar and too much liquid in the jam and it has been stored incorrectly.

Solution: If your jam has less sugar than an equal weight to fruit ratio, then always store it in a cool. dry place and use it within a reasonable period of time.

There is mould growing either on the top or round the sides of the jam.

Reason: This is most likely due to a poor seal on the jar and / or potting the jam when barely warm, so that airborn spoiling organisms were able to land on the jam.

Solution: Pot and seal your preserve whilst still hot and make sure that the lid is very secure.

My jam is coming away from the sides of the pot.

Reason: This is probably due to shrinkage of the jam. The liquid in the jam has evaporated away from the jam through the lid.

Making Jams and Preserves

Solution: It is probably the seal that is at fault, so make sure that all the jars used have a tightly fitting lid and that the preserve is stored in a cool, dark place.

My jam just won't set.

Reason: This is usually down to a lack of pectin in the mixture, or too much sugar being added in relation to the pectin and acid content.

Solution: Make sure that you measure the correct amount of sugar as stated in the recipe and check whether the fruit you are using has a high or low pectin content. Even if you stick to a recipe the result still depends on the fruit you have used at that time. After 10 minutes or so of boiling, or whatever is stated in the recipe, you could try adding a sachet of pectin and boiling for just 4 minutes. If it isn't setting as it should, don't keep boiling and boiling or it will be inedible. Pot it as it is and use it as ice-cream and desert sauce.

There are lots of crystals in my jam.

Reason: This is usually because the acid content of the jam is either too low or has been added after the sugar and boiled for too long.

Solution: Check the recipe regarding adding the acid (usually lemon juice) and add when cooking the fruit, not with or after adding the sugar.

Chapter Four
Marmalade

Marmalade is prepared in a similar way to jam in that the fruit is cooked and then boiled with sugar to a setting point.

Generally only citrus fruit is used in the making of marmalade. though the term is used in the making of other preserves such as onion mamalade. Every part of the fruit is used and, because the pips have a high pectin content, they are used in the cooking but lifted out before the sugar is added. This is done with a muslin bag or a secured square of cheesecloth.

Even though oranges and other citrus fruits have a high acidity level, they don't necessarily contain enough to make certain that the preserve will set. This is because citrus fruits produce a high yield of preserve in relation to the weight of fruit. So our friend the lemon is used once again to ensure a perfectly set marmalade.

The pith, which also contains a high amount of pectin, and peel are all cooked together with the juice and the flesh of the fruit. Because the peel is so tough, the cooking time of the fruit is longer. The peel must be cooked until it almost disintegrates when pressed with a spoon.

The best and easiest to make orange marmalade is made from bitter oranges. These are the famous Seville oranges that have a very short season. The fruit has a rough looking skin that is a deep orange in colour. They are not suitable for eating raw as the flesh is very bitter, but they do make perfect marmalade. They are only available in December and January, so January is the month to make your marmalade. If you have a glut of oranges they will freeze well and can be made into marmalade very successfully at any time. They are best frozen whole. Wash and dry them well, then place them into a food bag and freeze immediately. They may also be cooked as in step 2 of the Seville Orange Marmalade recipe, then cooled thoroughly and frozen in containers. The pectin content of the fruit will, however, diminish during freezing, so use either more fruit than is needed in the recipe (about an 1/8th more) or use a sachet of pectin in the boiling process.

Seville oranges are not the only citrus fruit used to make marmalade. Lemons, limes, grapefruits, mandarins, clementines and tangerines all make delicious preserves. Tangerine marmalade is wonderful at Christmas time. Combinations of fruit are also delicious and other flavours such as spices, spirits and liqueurs make a jar of preserves into a very special gift or a family treat. ❧

Things to remember when making marmalade.

• Choose fruit that is firm and has a good, bright colour.

• Scrub the fruit with a sponge and a little soap to remove any grease and rinse well.

• Make the marmalade as soon after purchasing the fruit as possible to ensure the freshness, flavour and preserving quality.

• To prepare the fruit, cut it in half and remove the pips, catching the juice in a bowl. Remove the flesh and add it to the juice, then shred the pith and peel. The smaller the shreds, the quicker it will cook. I find it easier to get the size of shred required at this stage rather than messing around with hot peel later.

• If the fruit has very large areas of pith that you don't want in your finished preserve, then remove it from the peel and place it in the bag with the pips.

• As the cooking time is so long the fruit may be cooked in a pressure cooker if you have one.

• After the initial cooking time of the fruit has elapsed, remove the bag of pips and, using tongs or two spoons, squeeze the bag to extract all the pectin-rich juice back into the mixture.

Making Jams and Preserves

• As marmalade needs to be boiled longer than most jams it is best to test for the setting point somewhat later than described in the jams section, as well as using a thermometer. The setting point usually occurs after 15-20 minutes of boiling, so boiling for at least 15 minutes is advisable.

• Marmalade produces more scum than jam and this needs to be removed or it clings to the pith and spoils the clarity of the finished preserve. This can be done with a large spoon or spatula or a small knob of butter which will disperse the scum. To ensure an even distribution of peel, allow the marmalade to cool for 5 minutes before stirring and potting. The peel shouldn't then float to the top of the marmalade.

Grapefruit Marmalade

Makes approximately 2.5kg / 5lb

3 large grapefruits / 1 lemon
1.5kg / 3lb sugar
2 litres / 4 pints water

1. Pare the rind from the fruit and cut into fine shreds. Juice the grapefruit and put the juice and peel shreds into the pan with the water. Put the pips in a muslin bag.

2. Chop the rest of the fruit into chunks, removing large portions of the pith and put it into the bag with the pips. Leave to soak for 3 hours.

3. Simmer the fruit for 2 hours until the peel is soft.

4. Add warmed sugar to the cooked fruit and stir until it dissolves.

5. Boil for 20 minutes, then test for setting, continuing to boil if not ready. Keep testing every 5 minutes.

6. Remove the scum and leave to cool for 20 minutes before stirring and potting in prepared jars.

This should keep for up to a year.

Lemon Marmalade

Makes approximately 3kg / 6½lb
12 lemons
1.5kg / 3lb sugar
1.8 / 3 pints water

1. Scrub the lemons and peel off the rind, leaving the pith on the fruit. Cut the peel into shreds and place it in the pan with the water.

2. Juice the lemons and place them in the pan with the water and peel. Chop up the rest of the fruit, cutting away any large pieces of pith. The rest will dissolve in the cooking. Put the pips and pith in a muslin bag. Put everything together in the pan with the water and simmer for 2 hours until the peel is tender.

4. Towards the end of the cooking time, warm the sugar. Remove the bag of pips.

5. Add the warmed sugar and stir until it dissolves. Bring the mixture to the boil and begin timing 15 minutes. After this test for setting, but continue to boil if it doesn't set.

6. Remove any scum as before and leave it to cool for 15 minutes. Stir before potting into prepared jars.

This should keep for up to a year.

Lemon and Lime Marmalade

Makes approximately 3kg / 6½lb
6 lemons and 6 limes
1.5kg / 3lb sugar
1.8 / 3 pints water

1. Scrub the lemons and limes and peel off the rind, leaving the pith on the fruit. Cut the peel into shreds and place it in the pan with the water.

2. Juice the lemons and limes and place them in the pan with the water and peel. Chop up the rest of the fruit, cutting away any large pieces of pith. The rest will dissolve in the cooking. Put the pips and the pith in a muslin bag. Put it all into the pan with the water and simmer for 2 hours until the peel is tender.

4. Towards the end of the cooking time warm the sugar. Remove the bag of pips.

5. Add the warmed sugar and stir until it dissolves. Bring the mixture to the boil and start timing 15 minutes. After this time test for setting, but continue to boil if it doesn't set.

6. Remove any scum as before and leave it to cool for 15 minutes. Stir before potting into prepared jars.

This should keep for up to a year.

Mixed Citrus Marmalade

Makes approximately 2.5kg / 5lb

1.5kg / 3lb mixed citrus fruit (including 2 lemons)
1.5kg / 3lb preserving sugar
3 litres / 6 pints water

1. Cut all the fruit in half and juice it. Place the juice in the pan with strips of lemon peel.

2. Cut all the remaining fruit into chunks and place it in the pan with the juice. Any pips can go into a muslin bag. Pour over the water and leave it to steep for 5 hours.

3. Cut the fruit into thin slices, putting any large chunks of pith in the bag with the pips.

4. Bring it to the boil and simmer for 2 hours until the peel is tender.

5. Add the sugar and allow it to dissolve before bringing it to the boil. Cook at boiling for 10-15 minutes until the marmalade reaches its setting point.

6. Allow it to cool for 10 minutes, then ladle it into jars.

This should keep for up to a year.

Old English Marmalade

This is the rich, dark marmalade that tastes amazing on any bread or in puddings.

The recipe is similar to the previous one except for the sugar, combining both brown and white together with a little dark treacle in the preparation.

Makes approximately 4.5kg / 9lb

1.5kg / 3lb Seville oranges
1kg / 2lb white sugar
1.5kg / 3lb brown sugar
1 tablespoon dark treacle
2.8 litres / 5 pints water

Prepare as before, but make sure that the brown sugar has dissolved completely as it takes a little longer than white.

This should keep for up to a year.

Orange and Ginger Marmalade

This recipe uses either frozen cooked pulp or a can of ready pulped oranges. It enhances the flavour of a ginger sponge cake and adds considerable zing to stewed rhubarb. I tend to use half brown and half white sugar as it gives a richer flavour and a deeper colour, but this is optional.

Makes approximately 3kg / 6lb

Either 1kg / 2lb frozen ready cooked
Seville oranges (thawed) or one 850g can
of prepared Seville oranges
1kg / 2lb sugar
220g / 8oz crystallised ginger, cut into
small pieces

1. Place the prepared oranges in the pan with the sugar on a low heat and stir until all the sugar has dissolved.

2. Add the ginger and bring it all to the boil. Cook at boiling for about 15 minutes or until the setting point is reached.

3. Allow it to cool for 10 minutes, then stir and ladle it into jars.

This should keep for up to a year.

Orange and Lemon Marmalade

Makes approximately 3kg / 6lb

3 oranges, either bitter or sweet
3 lemons
1.8kg / 4lb sugar
2.5 litres / 5 pints water

1. Scrub the fruit and cut in half. Remove the pips and place them in a muslin bag, catching all the juice in a bowl.

2. Chop the rest of the flesh into small chunks and the peel into thin strips. Place everything in the pan with the water and simmer for 2 hours until all the peel is tender.

3. Add the sugar and stir until dissolved. Bring to the boil and continue for 20 minutes. Check for setting in the usual way.

4. Allow it to cool for 5 minutes before potting.

This should keep for up to a year

Orange and Pumpkin Marmalade

Makes between 2-2.5kg / 4-5 lb

1kg / 2lb pumpkin flesh, cut into cubes
2 Seville oranges (or any type)
2 lemons
1kg / 2lb preserving sugar
400ml / 15fl oz water

1. Place the pumpkin into a bowl and add the juice of the 2 lemons.

2. Cut the oranges up, catching all the juice and putting all the pips into a muslin bag.

3. Put the oranges, lemon shells and water into a preserving pan and bring it to the boil, simmering for about 20-30 minutes until the peel is tender.

4. Add the pumpkin to the pan and cook with the oranges for a further 15-20 minutes until the pumpkin begins to pulp.

5. Add the sugar and stir it into the fruit. Keep stirring until all the sugar has dissolved.

6. Bring to the boil and cook as such for 15 minutes. Check for the setting point and cool it for 5 minutes. Stir and ladle into jars.

Quick Microwave Marmalade

2 medium oranges
1 lemon
500g / 1lb sugar
500ml / 18fl oz boiling water

1. Juice the lemon and remove the pips. Place them and the lemon shell in a muslin bag.

2. Slice the oranges into thin strips and place them with the juice into a large microwavable bowl.

3. Add the lemon juice and place the muslin bag in the centre. Cover with 300ml of boiling water. Leave to soak for 1 hour.

4. Add the remaining water and cook in the microwave on high for 20 minutes. Check the peel for tenderness and, if necessary, cook for a further 5 minutes. Remove the muslin bag, sqeezing out all the juice.

5. Stir in the sugar and cook on high for 10 minutes, then stop and stir. Now cook for 5 minutes and stir again, repeating the process for 20 minutes.

6. Test for setting allow it to stand for 10 minutes before ladling it into prepared jars and sealing.

This should keep for 9-10 months unopened.

Seville Orange Marmalade

Makes approximately 4.5kg / 9-10lb

1.5kg / 3lb Seville oranges
2.5kg / 5lb sugar
Juice of 2 lemons
2.8 litres / 5 pints water

1. Wash the fruit and cut it in half, retaining all the juice. Put the pips into a muslin bag. There will be a lot of them.

2. Remove all the flesh and pith and place it in the pan with the juice and the muslin bag of pips. Cut the peel into strips and place it in the pan. Add the water and simmer for approximately 2 hours. Test the peel for tenderness after this time. Remove the bag of pips, squeezing out all of the juice back into the pan.

3. Add the lemon juice and sugar and stir on a low heat until the sugar has all dissolved.

4. Bring to the boil and cook for 15 minutes. Test for setting and boil for longer if necessary.

5.Remove any scum and allow it to cool for 5 minutes. Stir just before potting and seal the jars in the same way as described in the jam section.

This should keep for up to a year.

Tangerine Marmalade

Use preserving sugar for this recipe as tangerines are a bit unpredictable in their pectin content.

This makes approximately 2.5kg / 5lb

1.5kg / 3lb tangerines
1.5kg / 3lb preserving sugar
4 lemons
2.8 litres / 5 pints water

1. Cut the fruit in half and squeeze out the juice, putting the pips in a muslin bag as before. Leave the lemons in halves, but slice the tangerines very thinly, especially the peel.

2. Put all the fruit and juice into a pan with the water and leave it to steep for 4½ – 5 hours. Bring the fruit and water mix to the boil and simmer for 1½ hours or until the peel is tender.

3. Remove the lemon peel and the bag.

4. Add the sugar, stirring all the time until dissolved. Bring to the boil again and cook at boiling for 15 minutes, after which test for setting.

5. When the setting point is reached, cool it for 5 minutes, then stir and ladle into prepared jars.

This should keep for up to a year.

Chapter Five
Making Jellies

Jellies are particularly good for those who are not fond of 'bits' in their jam and marmalade. They are richly coloured, clear, highly flavoured preserves that are a wonderful reminder of summer in the depths of winter. Their enjoyment, however, is not without cost as they take a lot more time to prepare and the yield of jelly to fruit is much lower than in jam making. This is because only the juice is used in the final cooking with the sugar and all the pulp, pith and rinds are discarded. On the plus side, though, it also means that you don't have to remove stalks or pips as this is simply done in the straining stage of preparation. If you dislike throwing away all the leftovers from the fruit it can, however, be used to make fruit cheese, in which case preparing the fruit, that is, hulling and peeling, must be done.

The equipment you use for jam making can also be used in the making of jellies. In addition you will need a reliable strainer. These can be purchased quite cheaply or you can make your own. I saw Mole making bramble jelly in an episode of my favourite children's program 'The Wind in the Willows.' He used an upturned, four legged stool as a frame for holding a jelly bag made from a large square of white cotton cloth. He had tied the four corners to each of the stool legs. The fruit was then poured into the makeshift bag and the juice collected in a bowl underneath. You can use a fruit press if you wish, but the juice must still be strained.

It is a job that requires patience as the juice takes some considerable time to trickle through the cloth, whether using a home-made or a bought jelly strainer. The temptation is great, but it MUST NOT be pushed through as this also forces some of the pulp through and causes a cloudy jelly. You can purchase a mechanical juicer that enables a quicker extraction of the juice. This is specially designed to steam cook the fruit and extract the clear juice at the same time. These are useful if you are going to make a large quantity of different fruit jellies.

You will also need a large measuring jug and in my experiencethe the bigger the better. You will need to measure your juice yield accurately because the amount of sugar in the recipe depends on the amount of juice produced after straining.

Suitable Fruit For Jelly Making.

Most fruits that can be used in jam making can also be used to make jellies, but as you will need a higher quantity of fruit than in jam making, it may be better to use home grown or wild fruits because of the cost. It is also good to choose fruits that give a good colour and set to the jelly. If a fruit has a low pectin content this can be added in the cooking of the jelly as it is important to have a good set. Here is a list of really good fruit to use in jelly making.

Cooking apples	Crab-apples	Bilberries
Blackberries	Blackcurrants	Gooseberries
Lemons	Limes	Loganberries
Oranges	Plums	Quinces
Redcurrants		

Other fruits can be made into jellies, like raspberries, but they will need extra pectin to help with the setting point.

Steps in Making Jellies

Step 1 - Preparing the fruit

Wash all the fruit thoroughly, even if it has been bought from the shops, as it mustn't have any grease or dust on it as this will spoil the finished jelly. Discard any obviously bruised or damaged fruit, or cut out the 'bad' parts of larger fruit. There is no need to hull or remove small bits of stalk as this will be removed in the straining process as mentioned earlier.

Step 2 - Cooking the fruit
Simmer the fruit with the correct amount of

water as stated in the recipe. Some fruits such as blackberries and loganberries won't need much water, but apples and quinces will need quite a substantial amount adding, usually enough to just cover the fruit.

Step 3 - Straining the cooked pulp

After cooking, the juices in the fruit will be running freely and the cooked pulp will be ready for straining. You will need your jelly bag, stand and a large bowl for catching the juice. When you have erected your jelly bag on its stand and placed the bowl underneath, pour the cooked fruit pulp into the straining bag. Leave the fruit to drain through the strainer for several hours.Some may even benefit from being left overnight as it takes a long time for this stage to be completed. I must stress, don't be tempted to squeeze the bag as this will certainly spoil the finished clarity of the jelly. With some fruits that are rich in pectin, such as gooseberries, cooking apples and red currants, you can take a second extraction of the juice. This is done by cooking the fruit with between half and two thirds of the water, then straining the pulp for about 30 minutes. After this initial straining the pulp is returned to the pan with the remaining water and simmered for a further 30 minutes. The pulp is then left to strain completely for several hours until no juice is dripping from the jelly bag. The juice must be used immediately as it will deteriorate very quickly after straining.

Making Jams and Preserves

Step 4 - Measuring the juice

This is very important as it is the way the amount of sugar is measured for that particular recipe. The amount of sugar needed depends precisely on the amount of juice extracted from the fruit. This may differ between batches of fruit used, so the juice must be measured before adding the sugar.

Step 5 - How much sugar do I need?

This depends on the type of fruit used; pectin-rich fruits will need 1kg of sugar for every single litre of juice or 1lb 4oz of sugar for every pint. For fruit with a medium pectin content, use 800g of sugar for every litre of juice or ¾lb of sugar to every pint. If you are using fruit with a low pectin content, use the amount of sugar needed for fruit with medium content but with the addition of some liquid or powdered pectin. For every kilo of sugar used, add one sachet or 100ml of liquid pectin, unless stated differently in the recipe. White sugar gives the clearest jelly.

Step 6 - Adding the sugar

Put the juice back in the preserving pan and bring to the boil. As the juice is coming to the boil warm the sugar as described in the jam section. When the juice is boiling, reduce the heat and simmer gently, adding the sugar and stirring gently until it has all dissolved. Any stirring at this stage must be done gently as bubbles will form in the jelly if it is done too vigorously.

Warming the sugar aids the dissolving speed as it won't reduce the temperature when added.

Step 7 - Boiling and setting

When all the sugar has dissolved bring it back to the boil and cook at boiling for 8 minutes. Check for setting after this time and, if ready, remove it from the heat but, if not, then boil for a further 2 minutes, but no longer, or the jelly could become tough. The flake test, or cold saucer test, is the best way of checking, rather than using a thermometer. See the basic steps in chapter 3 for more details of testing for the setting point.

Step 8 - Removing the scum

After the setting point is reached, remove any scum from the top of the jelly using a large spoon, preferably one with holes in it so that you don't lose any of the jelly.

Step 9 - Potting the jelly

All jars and lids must be sterilized before use.

Warm the jelly jars and pour or ladle the jelly into them very slowly and carefully to avoid any bubbles forming in the jelly. Holding the jars at a tilt helps with this, but be careful as the jelly is very hot when it reaches the jar and can burn your hand, so protect them with a tea towel. Cover with a waxed disc before sealing if you are not using a screw top lid. Label and date your jelly before storing. Most jellies should keep for 6-9 months.

The Yield

This is very difficult to give as it depends on the types of fruit and how much juice is obtained on extraction. A rough guide in order to help you to sterilize the correct amount of jars is, for every 3kg / 6lb of sugar used, expect approximately 5kg / 10lb of jelly for most fruit types. ❦

Apple Jelly

3kg / 6lb cooking apples
Juice of 1 lemon
Sugar as described in Step 5
Enough water to just cover the fruit in
the pan.

1. Cut the apples into chunks or slices and place them in the pan. Pour over the water to just cover the fruit and simmer until pulped.

2. Strain the pulp as described in Step 3.

3. Measure the juice and weigh the sugar. Warm the sugar in a low oven, whilst bringing the juice back to the boil in the pan.

4. When the juice is boiling, turn down the heat and stir in the sugar.

5. Bring to the boil and cook at boiling for 5 minutes before testing for the setting point. Carry on boiling until the setting point is reached, then leave to cool slightly, skimming off any scum before potting.

Bilberry Jelly

3kg / 6lb bilberries
Juice of 2 lemons
430ml / ¾ pint water
Sugar
1 sachet pectin

1. Put the bilberries in the pan with the water and lemon juice and simmer until the fruit is soft.

2. Strain until all the juice has dripped through and measure the amount. Weigh the correct amount of sugar and warm as before.

3. Bring the juice to the boil and lower the heat before stirring in the sugar gently.

4. When the sugar is fully dissolved, bring to the boil again and continue boiling for 5 minutes. Test for setting as before.

5. Cool slightly and remove any scum before potting.

Blackberry Jelly

2.5kg / 5lb blackberries
500ml / 18fl oz water
Juice of 2 lemons
Sugar

1. Put the fruit, lemon juice and water in the pan and simmer until soft.

2. Strain and measure the juice.

3. Warm the sugar and bring the juice to the boil.

4. Reduce the heat and stir in the sugar. Allow the sugar to dissolve completely before bringing to the boil again.

5. Boil until the setting point is reached. Test for setting after 5 minutes.

6. Cool for a few minutes, remove any scum and pot immediately.

Blackcurrant Jelly

3kg / 6lb blackcurrants
1.3 litres/ 2½ pints water
Sugar

1. Cook the blackcurrants with two thirds of the water given in the recipe. Simmer until soft.

2. Strain the juice and store it. Place the fruit back in the pan with the remaining water and simmer for another 10 minutes. This will give a second extraction of juice. Strain until no more juice is dripping from the straining bag.

3. Measure all the juice, weigh the sugar and warm it in the oven.

4. Add all the juice to the pan and bring to the boil.

5. Reduce the heat and stir in the sugar. When it has dissolved bring back to the boil.

6. Continue to boil, testing for setting after 5 minutes.

7. When the setting point is reached, cool, remove any scum and pot immediately.

Blackberry and Apple Jelly

2kg / 4lb blackberries
1kg / 2lb cooking apples, chopped
1litre / 2 pints water
Sugar

1. Place the fruit in the pan with the water and simmer until the fruit is soft.

2. Strain the pulp and measure the juice. Weigh the appropriate amount of sugar and warm it gently.

3. Put the juice and sugar back into the pan and on a low heat, stir gently until all the sugar has dissolved.

4. Raise the heat and boil the mixture for 8 minutes, checking for the setting point.

5. Cool slightly, skim if necessary and pot immediately.

Crab-apple Jelly

3kg / 6lb crab-apples
Juice of 1 lemon
Enough water to cover the fruit
Sugar

1. Remove the stalks and cut the fruit into slices or chunks. Place the fruit, lemon juice in a pan and cover with water.

2. Cook at simmering until the fruit is soft. Crab-apples take a long time to tenderise.

3. Strain and measure the juice. Weigh the appropriate amount of sugar and warm in the oven.

4. Boil the juice and stir in the sugar. Reduce the heat until all the sugar has dissolved.

5. Bring back to the boil and cook at boiling until the setting point is reached. This should take about 4-5 minutes.

6. Leave to cool for a few minutes, remove any scum and pot.

Cranberry Jelly

1.5kg / 3lb cranberries
500ml / 1pint water
Sugar

1. Cook the cranberries in the water until very tender.

2. Strain the juice. Measure the juice yield and weigh the appropriate amount of sugar, then warm it in a low oven.

3. Put the juice in the pan with the sugar and stir over a gentle heat until all the sugar has dissolved.

4. Turn up the heat and boil for 10 minutes. Check for the setting point and, when ready, allow to cool slightly before potting.

Damson Jelly

2kg / 4lb damsons
Juice of 2 lemons
350ml / 12fl oz water
Sugar

1. Place the damsons in the pan with the lemon juice and water and simmer until tender. This may take 30-40 minutes.

2. Strain and measure the juice and weigh the appropriate amount of sugar. Heat this gently in the oven.

3. Bring the juice to the boil in the preserving pan, then turn down the heat and gradually stir in the warmed sugar. Stir gently until all the sugar has dissolved.

4. Boil for about 5 minutes, then check for the setting point, continuing to boil if necessary.

5. Allow it to cool for a few minutes and remove any scum before potting.

Elderflower Jelly

2kg / 4lb cooking apples
Juice of 3 lemons
20 elderflower heads, roughly chopped
75g sugar per 100ml liquid

1. Roughly chop the apples and place them in a saucepan with the elderflower heads along with just enough water to cover. Bring to the boil, reduce to a simmer and cook for 30 minutes until very soft.

2. Pour the mixture into a jelly bag and drain it into a bowl overnight.

3. The following morning discard the fruit, then measure the volume of the liquid and add 75g of sugar per 100ml of fluid.

4. Place the liquid and the lemon juice in a saucepan and heat it through, stirring until all the sugar is completely dissolved. Bring to the boil and cook rapidly for about 15 minutes.

5. Once the jelly has reached the setting point ladle it into sterilised jars and seal well.

Gooseberry Jelly

2kg / 4lb gooseberries
1 litre / 2 pints water
Sugar

1. Place the gooseberries in the pan with two thirds of the water and cook until tender.

2. Strain the fruit for at least 15 minutes, then return it to the pan and add the rest of the water. Simmer again for about 25-30 minutes.

3. Strain the pulp once more. This time leave it for at least 4 hours until all the juice has been extracted.

4. Measure the juice, weigh the appropriate amount of sugar and heat gently in the oven.

5. Bring the juice to the boil, turn down the heat and stir in the warm sugar.

6. Stir until all the sugar has dissolved, then bring it back to the boil.

7. Boil for 10 minutes before testing for setting.

8. When ready, remove from the heat and allow to cool, then remove any scum and pot.

Grape Jelly

This can be made with either green or black grapes or a mixture of both. They are cooked with an equal amount of cooking apples to give extra pectin and flavour.

500g / 1lb grapes
500g / 1lb cooking apples, diced
Juice of 1 lemon
300ml / ¼ pint water
Sugar

1. Place the grapes in the pan and crush them with a potato masher. Add the apples, water and lemon juice and cook for about 25-30 minutes until tender.

2. Strain the juice and measure the amount. Weigh the appropriate amount of sugar and heat gently in the oven.

3. Boil the juice, reduce the heat and stir in the sugar over a low heat until it has all dissolved.

4. Boil the mixture rapidly for 5 minutes, then test for the setting point. Keep checking until ready.

5. Remove from the heat and allow to cool slightly. Remove any scum and pot.

Haw Jelly

1.5kg / 3lb haw berries
1.2 litres / 2¼ pints water
Sugar

1. Put the haws in a pan and add the water. Cook until tender. This may take up to an hour.

2. Strain the juice and measure. Weigh the correct amount of sugar and warm gently in the oven.

3. Bring the juice to the boil and stir in the sugar. Remove from the heat and continue stirring until all the sugar has dissolved.

4. Boil the mixture for 15 minutes and test for the setting point. When the setting point is reached, turn off the heat and allow it to cool slightly before removing any scum and potting.

Herb Jelly

You can use any herb or combination of herbs in this recipe; sage goes well with pork and poultry, mint or rosemary with lamb and so on.

1kg / 2lb cooking apples
2 tablespoons of fresh herbs or 1 tablespoon of dried
Juice of 1 lemon
Sugar

1. Core and chop the apples and place them in a pan with sufficient water to just cover them. Add the lemon juice and half of the herbs.

2. Bring this to the boil, then simmer until the apples are very soft. Strain the juice without sqeezing using a jelly bag. Leave it for 3-4 hours. Measure the juice and weigh out 450g / 1lb sugar for every 575ml / 1 pint of juice.

3. Put the juice and the sugar in a pan and heat them gently until all the sugar has dissolved. Then bring it back to the boil and add the rest of the herbs. Boil it for 10 minutes or until the setting point is reached, then remove it from the heat.

4. Skim if necessary and stir it well to distibute the herbs evenly. Pot it in warm jars.

Lemon Jelly

1.5kg / 3lb lemons
2.8 litres / 5 pints water
Sugar

1. Pare off the rind and place it in a muslin bag.

2. Cut the rest of the fruit up into chunks, capturing as much of the juice as possible.

3. Pour over the water and place the bag of rind in the centre. Leave it to steep over-night.

4. Pour all the contents of the bowl into the pan and bring to the boil. Simmer and cook for 1½ hours or longer if the rind is still tough.

5. Strain the fruit, remove and save the bag of rind. The straining could take about 3 hours.

6. Measure the juice, weigh the appropriate amount of sugar and warm it.

7. Put the juice juice back into the pan, add the bag of rind and stir in the sugar.

8. Stir till the sugar has dissolved, then raise the heat and boil rapidly until the setting point is reached. Remove the bag of rind.

9. Allow it to cool slightly and pot immediately.

Mint and Apple Jelly

This is a quick and easy way to make a delicious accompaniment for roast meats.

3 tablespoons fresh mint, chopped
300ml /11 fl oz unsweetened apple juice
150ml / 5½ fl oz malt vinegar
500g / 1lb jam sugar

1. Put the apple juice and vinegar into the pan and bring them to the boil. Remove from the heat and stir in the sugar.

2. Stir until all the sugar has dissolved. Replace on the heat and bring to a vigourous boil. Cook at boiling for 4 minutes.

3. Remove from the heat and stir in the mint.

4. Allow it to cool for 10 minutes, then stir again to evenly distribute the mint. Pot it in warm jars.

Muscat Jelly

It was discovered over 200 years ago that combining the flavour of our very English gooseberry and elderflowers imitated the flavour of the very expensive Muscat wine.

2.5kg / 5lb gooseberries
Enough water to cover the fruit
10 elderflowers heads
Sugar

1. Cook the gooseberries in the water for about 25-30 minutes until soft. Strain the juice and measure.

2. Put the flower heads into a muslin bag.

3. Weigh the appropriate amount of sugar and heat gently in the oven.

4. Put the juice into the pan and heat gently. Add the warm sugar and stir until dissloved.

5. Bring to the boil and cook at boiling for 5 minutes. Add the flower heads to the mixture and cook for a further 5 minutes until the setting point is reached.

6. Remove the flower heads and allow to cool slightly before skimming and potting.

Orange Jelly

1.5kg / 3lbs Seville oranges
2 lemons
4 litres / 7 pints water

1. Pare off the rind and place in a muslin bag.

2. Cut the rest of the fruit up into chunks, capturing as much of the juice as possible.

3. Pour over the water and place the bag of rind in the centre. Leave to steep overnight.

4. Pour all the contents of the bowl into the pan and bring to the boil. Simmer and cook for 1½ hours, or longer if the rind is still tough.

5. Strain the fruit and remove and save the bag of rind. The straining could take about 3 hours.

6. Measure the juice, weigh the appropriate amount of sugar and warm it gently.

7. Put the juice juice back into the pan, add the bag of rind and stir in the sugar.

8. Stir in the sugar until it has dissolved, then raise the heat and boil rapidly until the setting point is reached. Remove the bag of rind.

9. Allow to cool slightly and pot immediately.

Raspberry Jelly

2kg / 4lb raspberries
Juice of 1 lemon
600ml / 1 pint water
330g / ¾lb sugar for every pint of juice
1 sachet pectin

1. Cook the raspberries with the lemon juice and water until the fruit is soft.

2. Strain and measure the juice. Weigh the appropriate amount of sugar and warm gently.

3. Place the juice, sugar and pectin in the pan and stir over a low heat until all the sugar and pectin have dissolved.

4. Bring to the boil and continue to boil for 4 minutes, then test for setting.

5. When ready, allow it to cool, remove any scum and pot.

Red Currant jelly

2kg / 4lb red currants
600ml / 1 pint water
Sugar

1. Put the fruit in the pan with the water and cook it for 25-30 minutes until the currants are tender.

2. Mash the currants to release the juice and strain the fruit.

3. Measure the juice, weigh the appropriate amount of sugar and warm it gently.

4. Put the juice and the sugar together in the pan and heat them gently, stirring carefully until all the sugar has dissolved.

5. Bring to the boil and cook at boiling for 10 minutes. After this time test for the setting point.

6. When ready, skim and pot.

Rosehip Jelly

1kg / 2lb rosehips
500ml / 1 pint water
Sugar

1. Cook the hips in the water until tender and strain the juice.

2. Measure the juice and weigh the appropriate amount of sugar. Warm this gently in the oven.

3. Place the juice and sugar in the pan and stir on a low heat until all the sugar has dissolved.

4. Bring to the boil and maintain this for 8-10 minutes until it reaches the setting point. Skim and pot.

Sloe and Apple Jelly

1kg / 2lb sloes, pricked with a fork
2kg / 4lb cooking apples, chopped
Juice of 1 lemon
Water to cover
Sugar

1. Cook the sloes with the lemon juice and enough water to just cover them. Simmer for 20 minutes, then add the apples and cook the two together until both are pulpy.

2. Strain the fruit and measure the juice. Weigh the appropriate amount of sugar and warm it gently.

3. Put the juice and sugar into the pan and heat gently, stirring until all the sugar has dissolved.

4. Bring back to the boil and cook at boiling until the setting point is reached. This could take any time between 5 and 12 minutes.

5. Allow to cool slightly, then skim and pot.

Spiced Apple Jelly

3kg / 6lb cooking apples
Juice of 1 lemon
Sugar as described in Step 5
1 cinnamon stick
6 cloves
Enough water to just cover the fruit in
the pan.

1. Cut the apples into chunks or slices and place them in the pan together with the cinnamon and the cloves. Pour over sufficient water to just cover the fruit and simmer until pulped.

2. Strain the pulp as described in Step 3.

3. Measure the juice and weigh the sugar. Warm the sugar in a low oven, whilst bringing the juice back to the boil in the pan.

4. When the juice is boiling, turn down the heat and stir in the sugar.

5. Bring to the boil and cook at boiling for 5 minutes before testing for the setting point. Carry on boiling until the setting point is reached, then leave to cool slightly, skimming off any scum before potting.

Spiced Bramble Jelly

2kg / 4lb blackberries
Juice of 2 lemons
100ml / 3fl oz water
Ground mixed spice (1 level teaspoon for
every pint of juice)
Sugar

1. Cook the blackberries with the lemon juice and water until tender.

2. Strain, measure the juice, weigh the appropriate amount of sugar and measure out the ground mixed spice.

3. Warm the sugar gently in the oven and heat the juice to boiling.

4. Turn down the heat and add the sugar and spice, stirring until completely dissolved.

5. Bring it back to the boil and continue to boil for 15 minutes or until the setting point is reached.

6. Pot immediately.

Strawberry and Apple Jelly

2kg / 4lb strawberries
1kg / 2lb diced, unpeeled cooking apples
750ml / 1¼ pints water
Sugar

1. Put the fruit into the pan with the water and simmer until the apple has reduced to a pulp.

2. Strain the fruit and measure the juice. Weigh the correct amount of sugar and warm it gently.

3. Put the juice and sugar into the pan and heat them gently, stirring carefully until all the sugar has dissolved.

4. Bring back to the boil and cook at boiling for 5 minutes. Test for setting.

5. When the setting point is reached, cool it slightly and skim. Pot immediately.

Things that may go wrong

Most of the problems are similar to those that could happen when making , but these are problems associated only with jellies.

There is very little flavour in my jelly.

Reason: This is due to over , either at the cooking of the fruit stage, or after adding the sugar.

Solution: Don't over boil the fruit or jelly. Cook the fruit until it is just soft and boil the jelly only until the boiling point is reached.

My jelly is cloudy.

Reason: This is because some of the pulp has squeezed through as well as the juice during the straining process.

Solution: Don't force the juice through the straining bag and make sure there are no holes in the bag as even a tiny tear can allow pulp through.

Chapter Six
Fruit Butters, Cheeses and Curds

I remember my Mother asking me as a child if I wanted lemon or jam Swiss roll. What she actually meant was did I want a Swiss roll spread with lemon curd or jam. I was always spoilt for choice as I liked both, but usually I went for the lemon cheese option.

But what is the difference between all the preserves?

Fruit Butters

These are made with the the fruit in a cooked, pulped state. They have half as much sugar as jellies and jams, which is simmered with the fruit until the mixture looks thick and creamy. Testing for a setting point isn't necessary as it is the consistency that denotes whether or not the butter is ready.

They only keep for about 3-4 weeks unopened, so they are best made in small amounts. Once opened they will keep for 5-7 days if refridgerated.

Fruit Cheeses

Cheeses are made in a similar way, but with more sugar. They require approxmately the same amount as jellies. Again it is the consistency that matters and not the setting point. The finished cheese needs to be thick and creamy. This is done by the simmering of the fruit and sugar. As the water evaporates from the mixture this results in a thickened consistency. This will taste at its best after 2 months, so it is best left to stand for that period of time. It should keep unopened for 6-8 months, but, once opened, should be used within 2 weeks and stored in the fridge.

Fruit Curds

These are made from the fruit with eggs and butter added to enrich the flavour and thicken the consistency.They are prepared in a different way to the other preserves. Because of their egg content and a lack of boiling their shelf life is much shorter. They are best refridgerated even when unopened. Use within 4 weeks of making.

Basic Steps

Most types of fruit are suitable for making butters and cheeses and, because there is no worry about a setting point, the pectin content isn't an issue in the preparation of these preserves. The sterilizing of jars and lids is, however, just as important for these preserves as with jams. This is because they are simmered and not boiled at the final stage of preparation, so cleanliness is of the utmost importance.

Clear labelling of jars is also important as their shelf life is shorter, so I would write on the label the date prepared and also the date by which the preserve must be consumed. This takes any guess work out of the freshness of the contents and helps the recipient, if they are given as a gift.

Equipment

The only additional equipment you will need besides all your other preserving equipment is a fine nylon or plastic sieve. Do not use a metal sieve as the acid in the fruit will react badly to metal.

Steps 1, 2 and 3 are the same for both cheeses and butters.

Step 1 - Preparing the Fruit.

All fruit must be thoroughly washed and any bad or bruised sections removed. Cut any larger fruit into smaller pieces, but don't bother discarding stems, stones or cores and there is no need to peel the fruit.

Fruit Butters, Cheeses and Curds

Step 2 - Cooking the Fruit

To help with the flavour and the texture of the cheese or butter some fruits which are low in acid will need extra lemon juice. This will be made clear in the recipe, but the following fruits are included in this category; dessert apples, bilberries, cherries, blackberries, peaches, quinces, pears, raspberries and strawberries. Use just enough water to cover the fruit, though some may need more. This will be explained in the recipe. Simmer the fruit until it is very soft.

Step 3 - Straining the Fruit

When the fruit is soft, rub it through the sieve into a bowl. As you will need to weigh this pulp it is a good idea to put it straight into the bowl in which you will weigh it.

Step 4 - Cooking the Fruit

Fruit cheese - After weighing the pulp, calculate how much sugar you will need, allowing for equal amounts of sugar to pulp. Put the fruit back into the preserving pan. If it is very juicy then bring it to the boil and reduce it by cooking away some of the liquid. Otherwise, add the sugar and stir on a low heat until all the sugar has dissolved. Simmer it for between 30 minutes and an hour, depending on the fruit type. Stir constantly. When most of the liquid has evaporated and the

Making Jams and Preserves

mixture is thick and creamy, it is ready. To check this, simply draw the spoon across the base of the pan. It should leave a clean line that doesn't disappear as soon as it is made.

Fruit Butters - After weighing the pulp, calculate how much sugar is needed. For butters this is half of the weight of the pulp, so if the pulp weighs 1kg use 500g of sugar. Put the pulp and the sugar in the pan and heat them on a low light until all the sugar has dissolved, stirring constantly. Then raise the heat slightly so that the mixture simmers. Continue this until it becomes thick and creamy. It is then ready for potting.

Step 5 - Potting and Storing

They are both best stored in small jars, as once opened they need to be consumed fairly quickly, usually within a week. Traditionally, fruit cheeses were potted in small moulds and turned out on small plates before serving. But all jars must be warm when the preserve is poured in. To aid both sterilization and the storing quality of butters, place the jars in hot water and bring to the boil, keeping them at boiling for 5 minutes. Fruit butters must be sealed well and as airtight as possible and are best kept in the fridge. Fruit cheeses actually taste better if kept for 6-8 weeks before consumption. They also need to be well sealed. Screw top lids and are best for both butters and cheeses, if possible.

Apple Butter

1.5kg / 3lb cooking apples
500ml / 1pint water
500ml / 1pint cider
Sugar

1. Chop the apples and cook them in the pan with the water and the cider. Simmer until the apples are soft.

2. Rub the fruit through the sieve, collecting all the pulp and juice. Measure the amount and weigh the appropriate amount of sugar (half the weight of the fruit).

3. Return the fruit pulp to the pan and simmer it for 15 minutes, then add the sugar and stir until it has all dissolved. Cook until the mixture has thickened and looks creamy. Pot it when still hot in warm jars.

For a spiced version of this recipe, add a teaspoon of mixed spice and half a teaspoon of cinnamon to the pulp when adding the sugar.

Blackcurrant Butter

2kg / 4lb blackcurrants
2 litres / 4 pints water
Sugar

1. Put the fruit into the pan with the water and simmer until soft.

2. Rub through a sieve and measure the pulp and juice. Weigh the sugar.

3. Put the fruit back into the pan and bring it back to the boil.

4. As soon as it is boiling, turn down the heat and add the sugar. Stir until it is all dissolved.

5. Simmer gently until thick and creamy and pot it into warm jars.

Gooseberry Butter

2kg / 4lb gooseberries
450ml / ¾ pint water
Sugar

1. Put the fruit into the pan with the water and simmer until soft.

2. Rub through a sieve and measure the pulp and juice. Weigh the sugar.

3. Put the fruit back into the pan and bring back to the boil.

4. As soon as it is boiling, turn down the heat and add the sugar. Stir until it is completely dissolved.

5. Simmer gently until thick and creamy and pot it into warm jars.

Plum Butter

1kg / 2lb plums
100ml / 3fl oz water
Sugar

1. Halve the plums and remove some of the stones. Crack them open and cook the kernels together with the fruit. Leave the other stones in the fruit.

2. Simmer in the water until tender and, when cooked, rub through the sieve. Weigh the pulp and measure out the appropriate amount of sugar.

3. Simmer the pulp until some of the juice has evaporated and add the sugar. Stir until it is completely dissolved.

4. Bring it back to the boil and cook for 2 minutes at boiling, then reduce the heat and stir constantly at simmering until it becomes thick and creamy.

5. Put it into warm jars.

Tomato and Marrow Butter

1 medium sized marrow, cut into chunks
1kg / 2lb tomatoes, ripe or still slightly
green
Juice of 2 lemons
Sugar

1. Simmer the marrow and the tomatoes together with the lemon juice until tender.

2. Rub the mixture through a sieve and weigh the pulp.

3. Measure the appropriate amount of sugar.

4. Put the pulp back into the pan and boil it for 2 minutes. Lower the heat and stir in the sugar, stirring gently but well until it has all dissolved.

5. Simmer until the mixture is thick and creamy and pot it into warm jars.

Apple Cheese

This is prepared in exactly the same way as apple butter, but when weighing the sugar, allow the same weight of sugar to fruit pulp and make sure that all the sugar has dissolved before boiling for 3 minutes. Simmer gently until all the liquid has evaporated and the cheese is thick and creamy.

Blackberry and Apple Cheese

1kg / 2lb blackberries
500g / 1lb cooking apples
400ml / ¾ pint water
Sugar

1. Roughly chop the apples and put them into the pan with the blackberries. Simmer for 20-25 minutes until the apples are pulpy.

2. Strain through a sieve and weigh the pulp.

3. Measure the amount of sugar required.

4. Put the pulp back into the pan and heat gently with the sugar, stirring until it has all dissolved.

5. Bring it back to the boil for 4 minutes, then reduce the heat to simmering and stir continuously until thick and creamy.

6. Pot it into warm jars.

Damson Cheese

3kg / 6lb damsons
300ml / ½ pint water
Sugar

1. Simmer the fruit with the water until soft. Rub them through a sieve and weigh the pulp.

2. Measure the right amount of sugar.

3. Put the pulp back into the pan and simmer until most of the liquid has evaporated.

4. Stir in the sugar and continue until all the sugar has dissolved.

5. Boil for 3 minutes, then pot it into warm jars.

Quince Cheese

1kg quinces
Juice of 1 lemon
Water to just cover the fruit
Sugar

1. Chop the fruit roughly and put it into the pan with the lemon juice and just cover it with water. Cover the pan and simmer until the quinces are soft.

2. Sieve the fruit and weigh the pulp.

3. Put the pulp and sugar back into the pan and heat gently, stirring well until all the sugar has dissolved.

4. Bring it back to the boil and cook at boiling for 4 minutes. Turn down the heat and simmer until thick and creamy. Pot it into warm jars.

Rhubarb Cheese

2kg / 4lb rhubarb
Juice of 2 lemons
200ml / 7fl oz water
Sugar
1 teaspoon ground ginger (omit this if
you wish)

1. Cut the rhubarb into 1cm pieces and put it into the pan with the lemon juice and water.

2. Stew until soft. It might be best to cover the pan with a lid. This could take 25-35 minutes.

3. Rub the pulp through a sieve and put it back into the pan to reduce at boiling for 5 more minutes.

4. Weigh the pulp and measure the appropriate amount of sugar. Put both back into the pan. Heat them gently until all the sugar has dissolved, stirring all the time. Add the ginger.

5. Bring it back to the boil and cook at boiling until very thick and creamy. Pot it into warm jars.

Apricot Curd

180g / 6oz dried apricots
225g / 8oz caster sugar
50g / 2oz butter
Juice of 1 lemon
2 eggs

1. Put the apricots in a bowl and cover them with warm water. Leave to soak for 24 hours.

2. Cook the apricots in the water in which they were soaked and simmer until tender. Liquidise them in a blender or a food processor.

3. Put the pulped apricots and the sugar into a double boiler or a bowl over a pan of boiling water and stir until all the sugar dissolves.

4. Add the butter and lemon juice and stir it to melt the butter.

5. Remove it from the heat and beat the eggs. Once beaten, pour them carefully into the apricot mixture and stir.

6. Put them back on the heat and stir until the curd thickens.

7. Pot and seal. Label with a use by date. 2 weeks will be about right and safe.

Lemon Curd

4 lemons
225g / 8oz butter
5 eggs
450g / 1lb caster sugar

1. Finely grate the peel of the lemons and extract all the juice. Place this in the double boiler or a bowl over a saucepan of boiling water.

2. Add the butter and sugar and stir gently until all the sugar has dissolved.

3. Beat the eggs. Remove the pan from the heat and stir in the eggs.

4. Place the pan back on a low heat and stir until the mixture thickens to the consistency of thick cream.

5. Pot it and label clearly with the date made and a best before date. If refridgerated it will keep for up to 4 weeks unopened but only for 2 weeks if kept in the cupboard unopened. Once opened use it within 7 days and store it in the fridge.

Orange Curd

4 oranges
225g / 8oz butter
5 eggs
450g / 1lb caster sugar

1. Finely grate the peel of the oranges and extract all the juice. Place them in the double boiler or a bowl over a saucepan of boiling water.

2. Add the butter and sugar and stir gently until all the sugar has dissolved.

3. Beat the eggs. Remove the pan from the heat and stir in the eggs.

4. Place pan back on a low heat and stir until the mixture thickens to the consistency of thick cream.

5. Pot it and label clearly with both the date made and a best before date. If refridgerated it will keep for up to 4 weeks unopened but this reduces to 2 weeks if kept in the cupboard unopened. Use it within 7 days once opened and store it in the fridge.

Chapter Seven
Celebration Preserves and Conserves

These are preserves that have a little luxury about them; a special treat or a gift for someone special. Some are very simple to make and follow the basic steps used in previous chapters, but others are a little more complicated and will take more planning.

The first few recipes have Christmas in mind and are good to make for the festive season. Mincemeat is a very traditional ingredient and a store cupboard necessity as Christmas approaches. The first recipe doesn't contain any nuts and so is good for those who prefer their mince pies made this way.

Easy Mincemeat with Brandy

450g / 1lb cored and diced cooking
apples
225g / 8oz vegetarian suet
280g / 10oz soft brown sugar
1kg / 2lb 2oz mixed dried fruit (raisins,
currants and sultanas)
110g / 4oz glace cherries, halved or
quartered, whichever you prefer
½ teaspoon mixed spice
½ level teaspoon cinnamon
Zest and juice of 1 lemon
5 tablespoons brandy

1. Stew the apples gently on a low heat until just tender. Don't add any water. Leave to cool.

2. Meanwhile, mix all the other ingredients together, making sure they are all well coated in the brandy.

3. Stir in the cooled apples and combine well with the other ingredients.

4. Put into prepared jars and seal well. Label and date them.

This should keep for 6 months and will certainly taste better if you leave it to mature for two weeks.

Mincemeat with Almonds, Amaretto and Rum

700g / 1½ lb diced and cored cooking apples
1kg / 2lb 2oz mixed dried fruit
110g / 4oz glace cherries, halved
450g / 1lb vegetarian suet
450g / 1lb soft brown sugar
Zest and juice of 2 lemons
80g / 3oz ground or flaked almonds
1 level teaspoon mixed spice
4 tablespoons Amaretto
6 tablespoons dark rum

1. Put the dried fruit and cherries into a large mixing bowl. Stir in the almonds and sugar. Pour over the lemon juice, zest, amaretto and rum. Stir well so all the fruit is coated. Cover with a cloth. Leave it overnight for the flavours to sink in.

2. The next day cook the apples on a low light until just soft and leave to cool.

3. Stir the dried fruit mixture, sprinkle over the spice and stir in the suet and cooled apples. Combine well, making sure the suet is evenly distibuted throughout the mincemeat.

4. Place it in prepared jars, seal and label. Leave it to mature for at least 2 weeks.

Hodgkin

This is a very different type of preserve. There is no boiling or cooking involved at all. It is both a drink and a dessert. Its name comes from a 15th century phrase 'hodge-podge' which means mixture.

The preparation of this starts in summer and ends after the last fruits of autumn have been collected. The first fruits in the layer are strawberries and raspberries. These are covered with brandy and a sprinkling of sugar. This is left until the next fruit layer is added and covered with spirit and so on until the months of fruit layers finishes with a topping of brandy and sugar. This is covered or sealed with a lid and left to mature for 2-3 months. The liquor may then be drunk and the fruits eaten with cream or whatever you fancy. You will need a large stone or glass jar that can be sealed.

All the fruit used must be just ripe and perfect. Wash it all well and dry everything before adding it to the jar. Approximately 200g / 8oz of each fruit is sufficient.

To prepare the hodgkin you will need a selection of fruit. Over the page I've listed some fruits that can be used and how to prepare them.

Strawberries	Hulled and halved
Raspberries	Hulled
Cherries	Stoned
Blackberries	Hulled
Peaches	Stoned and quartered
Apricots	Stoned and halved
Plums	Stoned and halved
Damsons	Stoned and halved
Dessert apples	Cored and thickly sliced
Pears	Cored and quartered

You will also need sufficient brandy to cover the fruit. This will depend on how big your final hodgkin is. Cheap brandy actually gives the best flavour to the preserve, so don't spend a fortune on the best spirit.

As you layer up the hodgkin, sprinkle each layer with 2 tablespoons of white granulated sugar before pouring over the brandy until each layer is completely covered. Always cover the container in between preparing the layers.

Black Cherry Conserve

If you can get Morrello cherries for this recipe, all the better, but if not then dark cherries will do.

1.5kg / 3lb dark cherries
225g / 8oz redcurrant jelly
1.5kg / 3lb sugar
Juice of 1 lemon
2 tablespoons cherry brandy or kirsch

1. Pit the cherries, catching any juice and put it aside.

2. Put the redcurrant jelly into a pan with any juice from the cherries, the sugar and the lemon juice.

3. Heat it gently until all the sugar has dissolved. Then bring it to the boil. As soon as it is boiling add the cherries and simmer it for 10 minutes, stirring occasionally.

4. Remove it from the heat and stir in the cherry brandy or kirsch. Stir well and pot it immediately.

Peach and Brandy Conserve

1.5kg / 3lb ripe peaches, stoned
110g / 4oz flaked almonds
85g / 3oz halved glace cherries
1kg / 2lb 2oz sugar
Juice and zest of 1 lemon
5 tablespoons brandy
1 sachet powdered pectin

1. Cut up the peaches and place them in a pan with the almonds, cherries. lemon juice and zest and bring to the boil. Cook for 5 minutes, then lower the heat and stir in the sugar and pectin.

2. Stir until all the sugar has dissolved, then boil for 4 minutes.

3. Remove from the heat and stir in the brandy.

4. Pour it into prepared jars.

Plum Conserve

Try to make this with dark skinned plums, as this gives the conserve a wonderful colour.

2kg / 4lb plums
180g / 6oz seedless raisins
300ml / ½ pint water
100g / 4oz chopped almonds
5 tablespoons dark rum

1. Cut the plums in half and take out all the stones. Put the stones into a pan with the water and simmer for 10 minutes.

2. Put the plums and raisins in a pan with the water from the stones, straining the water as you pour it so that all the stones are removed.

3. Simmer the plums and raisins for 10 minutes. Add a little more water if the mixture looks dry, but no more than 2-3 tablespoons.

4. Add the sugar and stir until it is dissolved, then simmer for 10 minutes. Remove it from the heat and stir in the rum and almonds. Leave it to stand for 5 minutes before potting it into warm jars.

Raspberry Conserve with Framboise

Framboise is a raspberry liqueur and goes particularly well in this full flavoured preserve.

1.5kg / 3lb fresh raspberries
1.5kg / 3lb caster sugar
3 tablespoons Framboise

1. Place the sugar in an ovenproof dish and warm it for 15 minutes at a low temperature.

2. Meanwhile, put the raspberries in the pan on a very low heat and warm them through until the juices begin to run. Do not stir them.

3. Put the warm sugar in the pan with the fruit and bring it quickly to the boil, stirring gently but taking care not to break up the raspberries. Turn down the heat and simmer it for 2 minutes, then remove it from the heat and stir in the Framboise.

4. Pot it into warm jars.

Strawberry Conserve with Grand Marnier

1.5kg / 3lb whole strawberries
1.5kg / 3lb sugar
1 sachet powdered pectin
3 tablespoons Grand Marnier

1. Place the strawberries in a bowl and pour over the sugar. Mix carefully to avoid bruising the strawberries. Cover and leave them overnight.

2. The next day, put the whole lot in the pan with the pectin and slowly bring it to the boil. Stir carefully but constantly to help the sugar to dissolve. When the mixture is boiling, time 4 minutes, then remove it from the heat. Stir and leave it to cool for 15 minutes.

3. Add the Grand Marnier and stir well.

4. Pot it into prepared jars.

Winter Conserve

This is so called because it can be made in the dead of winter. It uses prunes, raisins and chopped nuts and tastes similar to plum jam, with the added luciousness of the nuts, raisins and brandy.

450g / 1lb no-soak prunes with all the
stones removed
450g / 1lb raisins
120g / 4oz chopped mixed nuts or
chopped almonds and hazlenuts
600g / 1lb 5oz sugar
600ml / 1 pint water
5 tablespoons brandy

1. Put the dried fruit, nuts and a tablespoon of the brandy into a bowl. Pour over the water and stir well. Leave it overnight for the fruit to soak up the flavour of the brandy and the water.

2. Next day, put all the soaking mixture into the pan and heat it gently. Stir in the sugar and keep stirring until it has all dissolved.

3. Bring it to the boil and cook it for 10 minutes until the liquid has thickened. Remove it from heat and stir in the remaining brandy.

4. Pot it into warm jars.

Chapter Eight
Chutneys, Relishes, and Ketchups

Chutneys are an excellent way of preserving both fruit and vegetables as they have the longest shelf life of all preserves. So long as all the jars are clean and have an excellent seal they can last for at least 1½ - 2 years. A chutney has a smooth texture and is usually made from finely chopped fruit and vegetables and an individual balance of spices and other flavourings, so that each recipe will be different. They are cooked for quite a long period of time, so the flavours are at their best when left to mature for several weeks before use. Any pungent, spicy flavour will mellow over time and the flavours balance and blend, so don't be tempted to try out your chutney too early as the taste will change for the better over time.

Steps in making chutney.

Step 1 - Preparing the fruit and vegetables

Wash everything well and remove the peel, cores and stalks. Chop everything very finely. A food processor is ideal for speeding up this stage.
Step 2 - Cooking the ingredients

Making Chutneys, Relishes and Ketchups

Some, such as blackberries, may need some pre-cooking as they will need to be sieved to remove the seeds. Usually all the ingredients are cooked together, though. The texture of a finished chutney should be both thick and moist.

Step 3 - Potting

Chutneys are put into the jars whilst still hot and sealed immediately. This produces a good seal that allows the preserve to be kept for a long period of time. Once sealed, leave it in the same place until cool, then store it in a cool, dark and dry place.

None of the following chutney recipes are mind -blowingly hot, or over pungent, so they should appeal to most chutney lovers. If, however, you want a more pungent flavour, the amounts of the hotter spices, like chilli or ginger, can be increased. It is advisable to make a trial batch first so that you can make sure it is edible. You may use spiced or un-spiced vinegar, that is up to you. Spiced vinegar will give a full flavour. It is difficult to give a yield for chutneys as it depends on the type and ripeness of the produce used, so the yield will be approximate.

Autumn Fruit Chutney

Makes 2kg / 4lb

1.5kg / 3lb mixture of apples, pears,
damsons and plums, all cored or stoned
and chopped finely
90g / 3oz stoned dates, chopped
90g / 3oz raisins
450g / 1lb onions, chopped finely
2 garlic cloves, crushed
230g / 8oz soft brown sugar
1 teaspoon allspice
1 teaspoon ground ginger
1 teaspoon ground white pepper
580ml / 1pint malt vinegar
1 teaspoon salt

1. Put all the ingredients into the pan and heat them slowly until all the sugar has dissolved. Stir constantly.

2. Bring it to the boil, then turn down the heat and simmer for 1 hour until the mixture has thickened but is still moist.

3. Stir and pot it immediately.

Allow it to mature for 2 weeks before using.

Beetroot and Apple Chutney

This chutney goes well with roast pork or goose, either served hot or cold with salads.

Makes 2kg / 4lb

1kg / 2lb beetroot, peeled and grated
700g / 1½lb cooking apples, cored and diced but not peeled
500g / 1lb onions, chopped finely
500g / 1lb raisins
1 tablespoon mixed spice
1 teaspoon ground ginger
1 kg / 2lb soft brown sugar
1 litre / 2 pints malt vinegar

1. Put all the ingredients into the pan and bring them slowly to the boil, stirring continuously until the sugar has dissolved.

2. Simmer for 1 hour, or until everything is tender and the chutney has thickened.

3. Pot it and seal it immediately.

Making Jams and Preserves

Cranberry and Apple Chutney

This is particularly delicious with Christmas meats and is a change from cranberry jelly.

Makes 2.5kg / 5lb

1kg / 2lb cranberries
1kg / 2lb cooking apples, peeled, cored and chopped
230g / 8oz onions
750g / ¾lb soft brown sugar
Juice and zest of 2 oranges
1litre / 2 pints malt vinegar
1 teaspoon allspice
1 teaspoon cinnamon
1 teaspoon ground ginger
½ teaspoon dry mustard powder
25g / 1oz salt

1. Put all the ingredients into the pan and heat them gently, stirring until the sugar dissolves.

2. Gradually bring them to the boil, stirring continuously.

3. When boiling, reduce the heat to a simmer and cook it for 45 minutes or until the mixture is thick, but not dry.

4. Stir well then pot it immediately.

Caponata

This is an Italian salad side dish a bit like a pickled ratatouille. It is eaten immediately, stored covered in the fridge for a week or frozen and stored for 3 months.

1 red and 1 green pepper, chopped finely
1 large aubergine, diced
2 red onions, chopped finely
2 sticks of celery, chopped
1 can Italian chopped tomatoes
110g / 4oz pitted green olives, chopped
2 tablespoons capers
5 tablespoons olive oil
½ teaspoon salt
2 tablespoons caster sugar
50g / 2oz pine nuts
150ml / ¼ pint white wine vinegar
1 tablespoon chopped basil

1. Pour the oil into a large pan and add all the vegetables, except for the olives and capers, and sprinkle with the salt. Heat gently for 20 minutes with a lid on the pan.

2. Add the tomatoes and cook on a low heat for 10 minutes, then add the remaining ingredients, except for the basil. Simmer for 15 minutes until the mixture thickens.

4. Stir in the basil just before serving.

Dried Fruit Chutney

This is a change from brown pickle and can be served with most cold meats and cheeses.

Makes 1kg / 2lb

120g / 4oz raisins
120g / 4oz sultanas
220g / 8oz no soak dried apricots, chopped
450g / 1lb cooking apples, cored and diced
1 teaspoon cinnamon
1 teaspoon mixed spice
½ teaspoon ground cloves
1 teaspoon salt
450g / 1lb soft brown sugar
580ml / 1 pint white vinegar

1. Put everything into the pan, except for the apples, and heat it gently, stirring until all the sugar has dissolved.

2. Simmer it for 15 minutes, then add the apples and simmer for 45 minutes, stirring occasionally.

3. When thickened, stir and pot it immediately.

Leave it to mature for 2 weeks before using.

Easy Pumpkin Chutney

1.25kg / 2½lb diced pumpkin
450g / 1lb tomatoes, peeled and chopped
250g / 8oz onions, chopped
50g / 2oz sultanas
750g /1½lb soft brown sugar
2 cloves garlic
2 teaspoons allspice
1 teaspoon black pepper
25g / 1oz fresh ginger, chopped finely
2 tablespoons salt
600ml / 1 pint white vinegar

1. Put all the ingredients into a heavy based pan and bring to the boil.

2. Turn the heat down and simmer, stirring continuously until all the sugar has dissolved, then leave it to simmer gently for about 40 minutes.

3. When everything is tender and the chutney is thick, ladle it into sterilized jars and seal well.

Store for at least 6 weeks before serving.

Green Tomato Chutney

1.8kg / 4lb green tomatoes, chopped
700g / 1½lb onions, sliced
450g / 1lb bramley apples,peeled, cored and
diced
575ml / 1pint white vinegar
450g / 1lb golden caster sugar
25g / 1oz fresh ginger, chopped
½ level teaspoon mixed spice
225g / 8oz raisins
2 teaspoons salt

1. Put the tomatoes, onions and apples into a large, heavy based pan with half of the vinegar and bring to the boil. Simmer until all are tender.

2. Add the spice, ginger and raisins and continue to simmer until the mixture is thick.

3. Add the salt, sugar and the rest of the vinegar and stir until the sugar has dissolved completely.

4. Cook on a low heat for about 1 hour until the chutney is thick.

5. Pour it into sterilized jars and seal well. Label them and leave to mature for at lest 5 weeks before eating.

Mixed Pepper Chutney

Try a little of this mixed with some grated mature cheddar cheese and toasted.

Makes 1.5kg / 3lb

2 each of red, green and yellow peppers, chopped finely
350g / 12oz tomatoes, chopped
350g / 12oz onions, chopped finely or minced in a processor
250g / 9oz soft brown sugar
1 teaspoon allspice
1 teaspoon dry mustard powder
1 teaspoon salt
½ teaspoon white pepper
480ml / 16fl oz malt vinegar

1. Put all the ingredients into a pan and simmer them together for 1½ hours. Stir constantly until all the sugar has dissolved, then just occasionally.

2. After the cooking time, check for the correct, thick consistency and pot and seal it immediately.

Mango Chutney

This is the classic accompaniment to curries and really sets off the spiciest of dishes. But it also goes well with cooked chicken.

3 green mangoes, diced into small cubes
4 cloves garlic, crushed
1 teaspoon freshly chopped ginger
350ml / 12fl oz white vinegar
350g / 12oz soft brown sugar
4 tablespoons sultanas
½ teaspoon turmeric
1 level teaspoon cayenne pepper
2 teaspoons salt for sprinkling on the mangoes
1 teaspoon salt

1. Put the diced mango into a dish and sprinkle it with salt. Cover and leave it overnight.

2. Rinse and dry it and place it in the pan with all the other ingredients. Bring them slowly to a gentle simmer, stirring all the time until the sugar has dissolved.

3. Continue to simmer for 30-40 minutes until the mixture thickens.

4. Pot it and seal the jars.

Pumpkin and Tomato Chutney

Makes 3kg / 6lb

1 medium sized pumpkin, peeled and cut
into small chunks
460g / 1lb red tomatoes, chopped
300g / 10oz onions, chopped finely
50g / 2oz raisins,
50g / 2oz sultanas
750g / 1½lb soft brown sugar
2 teaspoons ground ginger
2 teaspoons mixed spice
1 teaspoon cinnamon
1 teaspoon ground black pepper
2 cloves garlic, crushed
580ml / 1pint white vinegar
2 tablespoons salt

1. Put all the ingredients into the pan and heat them slowly until all the sugar has dissolved, stirring continuously.

2. Turn up the heat and bring it to boiling point, then turn down the heat and simmer it for 45-50 minutes until the chutney has thickened.

3. Stir and pot it immediately.

Leave it to mature for two weeks before using.

Quick Red Onion Chutney

This is a quick chutney that can be used as soon as it is cool and it goes really well with both burgers and sausages. This recipe makes a small amount but it can easily be doubled. A large, screw top jar is all you will need.

2 red onions, chopped finely or
processed
1 red pepper, chopped very small
5 tablespoons soft brown sugar
100ml / 3fl oz white wine vinegar
½ teaspoon salt
Pinch cinnamon
1 clove garlic, crushed

1. Put all the ingredients into a medium sized pan and heat them gently, stirring until all the sugar has dissolved.

2. Bring them to the boil, then turn down the heat and simmer for 45 minutes or until thick but moist.

3. Stir and pot it immediately.

This can be used as soon as it is cold. This cooling process can take several hours, so making the chutney the day before it is required is advisable.

Quick Sandwich Pickle

3 carrots,
1 medium swede,
4-5 garlic cloves,
10 dates,
2 onions
2 medium apples,
2 medium sized courgettes
250g / 10oz dark brown sugar
1 teaspoon salt
500ml / 1pint malt vinegar
2 teaspoons mustard seeds
2 teaspoons ground mixed spice

1. Finely chop all the vegetables.

2. Put all the vegetables, sugar, vinegar and spices into a large pan and bring them slowly to the boil.

3. When the pickle is boiling, reduce the heat and simmer for 1 hour, stirring occasionally. You can add a little water if the mixture is becoming too stiff.

4. When the vegetables are just becoming soft you can spoon the pickle into sterile jars.

Leave for 5-7 days for the flavours to mature.

Spiced Plums

1.3kg / 3lb plums
Grated rind and juice of 1 lemon
Grated rind and juice of 1 orange
1.3kg / 3lb sugar
6 cloves
1 stick cinnamon

1. Halve and stone the plums.

2. Put the plums in a bowl with the sugar and the orange and lemon rind. Mix in the juice and leave overnight.

3. Transfer it to a slow cooker. Add the cloves and cinnamon stick in a bag and cook for about 5 hours.

4. Remove the bag and pour in a little Drambuie for an added twist.

Store for about 3 months before serving.

Tomato Chutney

This is my favourite chutney for eating with burgers and hot dogs.

Makes 2kg / 4lb

1.5kg / 3lb chopped tomatoes
1 medium sized onion, finely chopped or processed
200ml / 7fl oz malt vinegar
200g / 7oz soft brown sugar
1 teaspoon mixed spice
½ teaspoon paprika
A tip of a teaspoon (optional) cayenne pepper
1 clove of garlic, crushed
1 level dessertspoon salt

1. Put all the ingredients into the pan with half of the vinegar. Simmer and stir it until the sugar is dissolved. Continue simmering for 30 minutes, then add the rest of the vinegar and simmer for 30-40 minutes, stirring occasionally.

2. If after this time the chutney hasn't thickened, continue to simmer until it reaches the desired thickness.

3. Pot and seal it immediately. Store it for 4 weeks before consuming and, once opened, refridgerate it and use it within a month.

Relishes

These are very easy to make, but they do need quite a bit of preparation. They don't keep as well as chutneys because they are not cooked for as long and they contain less sugar. But in a well sealed jar they will store for 3-4 weeks unopened in the refridgerator. They can be consumed as soon as they are cold, so no waiting around to taste them.

Beetroot Relish

A quick and easy relish to serve with salads and stews.

1kg / 2lb fresh beetroot, peeled and grated
500g / 1lb caster sugar
500ml / 1pint cider vinegar
1 teaspoon salt
½ teaspoon dried chilli flakes

1. Put all the ingredients into a pan and heat them gently until the sugar dissolves.

2. Bring it to the boil, then turn down the heat and simmer for 20 minutes.

3. Pot it immediately.

Hamburger Style Relish

Another one for barbecue time! This is easy to make and tastes much better than the shop bought variety.

230g / 8oz red tomatoes, chopped
2 red peppers, chopped finely
2 small onions, chopped finely
½ teaspoon dried chilli flakes
200g / 7oz caster sugar
2 tablespoons tomato ketchup
200ml / 7fl oz white vinegar

1. Put everything into the pan and heat it gently until all the sugar has dissolved.

2. Bring it to the boil, then simmer it for 20 minutes until thick.

3. Pot it immediately.

Quick Corn Relish

2 large cans sweetcorn, drained
2 small onions, chopped finely
1 red pepper, chopped finely
180g / 6oz caster sugar
½ teaspoon turmeric
2 teaspoons salt
1 teaspoon dry mustard powder
300ml / 10fl oz white wine vinegar
2 teaspoons plain flour

1. Put all the ingredients into a pan and sieve the flour evenly over them. Heat them gently to dissolve the sugar, stirring continuously.

2. Bring it to the boil and then simmer it for 10-15 minutes until thick.

3. Pot it immediately.

Tomato Relish

1.5kg / 3lb tomatoes, chopped
2 large onions, chopped finely
1 stick celery, chopped finely
1 small red pepper, chopped finely
350g / 12 oz caster sugar
1 dessertspoon mustard seeds
1 tablespoon sweet chilli sauce
300ml / 10fl oz white vinegar
25g / 1oz salt

1. Gently heat the vinegar, sugar, mustard seeds and salt in a large pan, stirring until all the sugar has dissolved.

2. Add the onions, celery and pepper, then bring it to the boil.

3. Turn down the heat and simmer it for 10 minutes.

4. Add the tomatoes and chilli sauce, then continue to simmer for 20 minutes until the mixture thickens.

5. Stir it well, then pot it immediately.

Leave it for 2 days before using.

Tomato Ketchup

Makes about 1.5 to 2 litres / 5 pints

3kg / 5lb plum tomatoes
2 small onions, finely chopped
3 level teaspoons salt
2 cloves garlic, crushed
½ teaspoon black pepper
½ teaspoon cayenne pepper
220g / 8oz sugar
300ml / 12fl oz cider vinegar
A finger sized cinnamon stick
5 whole cloves and 2 bay leaves

1. Peel your tomatoes and chop them into small pieces. Remove the seeds and skins.

2. Discard as much juice as you can; you can use it for other things. Place the tomatoes and a bag with all the spices into a pan along with the vinegar and simmer it for about 30-40 minutes.

3. Push the pulp through a sieve and discard the spices. Return the mix to the heat and gently simmer it for at least another 30 minutes to thicken the sauce.

4. Leave it to cool for 15 minutes, then pour it into glass bottles using a funnel. Seal them well.

This should keep for 2-3 months.

Tomato and Red Pepper Ketchup

Makes about 3 litres / 6 pints

3kg / 6lb red tomatoes, chopped
6 onions, chopped finely
6 red peppers, chopped finely
200g / 7oz soft brown sugar
2 teaspoons chopped root ginger
1 level teaspoon mixed spice
1 teaspoon cinnamon
½ teaspoon powdered cloves
3 teaspoons salt
1.5 litres / 3 pints white vinegar

1. Put the vinegar, spices, salt and sugar into the pan and heat them gently, stirring until all the sugar has dissolved.

2. Add the tomatoes, onions and peppers and bring them to the boil, then turn down the heat and simmer the mixture for 1 hour.

3. Rub through a sieve or blend in a processor.

4. Put it back into the pan and simmer it again until it is smooth and thick.

5. Pour it immediately into bottles using a funnel and seal well

This should keep for 2-3 months.

Mushroom Ketchup

Makes about 900ml / 1½ pints

900g / 2lbs mushrooms
56g / 2oz salt
½ teaspoon ground allspice
A pinch of ground mace
A pinch of ground ginger
A pinch of crushed cloves
A pinch of cinnamon
285ml / ½ pint malt vinegar

1. Wash and dry the mushrooms, trimming off the ends of the stalks if necessary, but do not peel them. Chop them into small pieces.

2. Layer the mushrooms in the salt in a large bowl. Cover and leave them for 24 hours and then rinse and drain.

3. Place them in a pan with the remaining ingredients and bring them to the boil. Reduce the heat and simmer for 30 minutes.

4. Strain through a sieve and pour it into hot, sterilized bottles and seal well.

Spicy Allotment Relish

225g / 8oz each of courgettes, carrots
and cauliflower
1 large onion
112g / 4oz each of sweetcorn & peas
1½ tablespoons salt
450 ml / ¾ pint cider vinegar
150ml / ¼ pint water
175g / 6oz soft dark brown sugar
1 teaspoon coriander seeds & ginger
½oz pickling spice
2 teaspoons curry powder
1 tablespoon cornflour

1. Dice the courgettes and onions, grate the carrot and break the cauliflower into florets. Put all the vegetables into a bowl, add the salt, mix and pour in just enough water to cover. Leave it to stand overnight. Drain well.

4. Combine the vinegar and sugar with the spices in a large pan. Add the pickling spice in a muslin bag. Boil and then simmer it for 20 minutes. Add the vegetables and simmer for 10 minutes. Bring it back to a fast boil and continue cooking for another 10 minutes. Remove the muslin bag.

Blend in the cornflour with 2 tablespoons (30 ml) of water and stir into the pan. Boil for 3 minutes. Ladle it into clean jars, cover and seal well.

Brown sauce

1.5kg / 3lb apples, cored and chopped
1.5kg / 3lb plums, stoned and chopped
2 onions, finely chopped
3 cloves of garlic, crushed
50g / 2oz salt
450g / 1lb dark brown sugar
1.5 litres / 3 pints malt vinegar
2 teaspoons ginger
2 teaspoons allspice
2 teaspoons nutmeg
1 teaspoon cayenne pepper

1. Finely chop the onions and garlic and add them to a large pan.

2. Add the fruit and boil it to a thick pulp in the vinegar. This needs to be puréed as much as possible by passing it through a sieve or by using a food processor.

3. Return it to the pan and add the spices. Reduce it on a low heat, mixing it well continuously.

When it has reached the thickness you like, pour it into sterile bottles. You will need to experiment with both the salt and sugar content as personal taste is the key to getting this recipe right.

This may be used as soon as it is cold and should keep for 6 months if unopened.

BBQ Sauce

A simple sauce for coating food like chicken or pork is easy to make. This isn't the type of sauce you would pour from a bottle onto a sandwich, but it can be used as either a dip or a marinade.

2 tablespoons sunflower oil
1 large finely chopped onion
1 tablespoon tomato purée or 2 tablespoons of ketchup as made above
2 tablespoons brown sugar
2 cloves garlic, crushed
1 large teaspoon mustard powder
2 tablespoons Worcestershire sauce (or try 2 tablespoons of the brown sauce recipe as above)
150ml / 5fl oz water
1 teaspoon salt

1. Heat the oil and cook the onions until transluscent.

2. Add all the other ingredients except the tomato, which should be added last and beaten well into the mixture. This doesn't require any more cooking as it is best used fresh. It will keep for two weeks in a srerile container in the fridge.

Green Tomato Sauce

2kg / 4lb green tomatoes, chopped
750g / 1½lb cooking apples, cored and
chopped
1 medium onion, chopped finely
280ml / ½ pint white vinegar
1 teaspoon pickling spices, ground
230g / 8oz soft brown sugar
2 teaspoon salt

1. Put all the ingredients into a pan and heat them gently, stirring until all the sugar has dissolved.

2. Bring it to the boil and reduce the heat. Simmer it for 45-50 minutes until pulpy and soft.

3. Rub through a sieve or put it into a processor and mix until smooth.

4. Return it to the pan and bring it to the boil.

5. Bottle it carefully using a funnel and seal it well.

This can be used as soon as it is cold and it stores for 3-4 months if unopened.

Sweet Chilli Sauce

15 ripe tomatoes
3 Bramley Apples
5 medium sized onions
2 red peppers
2 red chillies
4 cups white vinegar
1½ cups sugar
2 tablespoons pickling salt
1 tablespoon cinnamon
½ teaspoon ground cloves

1. Chop up the tomatoes, apples, onions, chillies and peppers.

2. Combine them in a large pot and add the remaining ingredients.

3. Bring it to the boil and cook until the sauce thickens.

4. Pour the hot sauce into sterilised bottles and seal well.

Chapter Nine
Making Fruit Syrups

Syrups are an excellent way of preserving the summer tastes of fruit and, as the only other ingredients are water and sugar, they are an inexpensive way to make a delicious sauce for ice-cream or puddings. They can also be used in drinks and, when diluted with an equal quantity of water, made into ice-lollies. Use them as a base for jellies and blancmanges too and as a milkshake syrup.

Use only ripe fruits that are in good condition. Anything else will spoil the flavour of the finished syrup. The basic method is the same for all the summer soft fruits; it is only the amount of water that is different.

Water Quantities

Blackberries - for every kilogram / 2lb of fruit add 100ml / 3fl oz of water.

Blackcurrants - for every 450g / 1lb of fruit add 280ml / ½ pint water.

Strawberries - for every kilogram / 2lb of fruit add 75ml / 2fl oz water

Raspberries- no water needed

Whatever quantity of fruit you use, remember that the yield will depend on the amount of juice that can be extracted from the fruit. Also, use heat minimally as this helps to keep the flavour of the fruit in the syrup.

Use white caster sugar or granulated as this gives the best fruit flavour. Golden and brown sugars give a caramelly taste that isn't unpleasant but does detract from the original flavour of the fruit.

Sugar Quantities

For a sweet syrup, ideal for topping ice-cream and desserts, allow 300g sugar to 500ml of juice (¾lb sugar to 1 pint of juice). These have the best keeping qualities. This syrup keeps for 6-8 weeks in the fridge.

For a less sweet syrup for making drinks and ice-lollies, allow 200g sugar to 500ml of juice (7oz sugar to 1 pint of juice). This keeps for 2-3 weeks in the fridge.

For a tangy sauce for drinks and cocktails, allow 100g sugar to 500ml of juice (3oz sugar to 1 pint of juice). This keeps for 5-7 days in the fridge.
1. Put the fruit and any water being used in the pan and bring them quickly to the boil. Cook for

Making Jams and Preserves

1 minute. Remove them from the heat and crush the fruit with a masher.

2. Use a jelly bag to strain the juice into a bowl and leave it overnight. The next day squeeze out any juice still left in the fruit.

3. Place the juice in the pan and weigh out the correct amount of sugar according to the type of syrup you wish to make.

4. Heat it gently without quite simmering and definitely not boiling. Add the sugar and stir until it is completely dissolved. Then remove it from the heat.

5. Pour it into sterilized bottles and seal them with a well fitting lid.

You can lengthen their shelf life by heating the bottles of juice in a large deep saucepan. This can be done by heating water to 78°C / 170° F and placing the sealed bottles in the water and heating the bottles for 30 minutes.

Alternatively, use a Campden tablet, used to purify wine. Simply add it to the syrup before bottling. Crush 1 tablet in a tablespoon of cooled, boiled water and stir it into the syrup, mixing it thoroughly before bottling.

Chapter Thirteen
Using Preserves

The wonderful thing about preserves, particularly jam and marmalade, is that they are a wonderfully versatile ingredient in so many other recipes. They can be used to thicken or sweeten sauces, as a base for pies and slices and as coatings for both cakes and roast meats. What would a Victoria sandwich cake be without a delicious jammy filling?

This chapter shows how you can use your home-made preserves both in a simple and familiar way, and also in more unusual and creative ways.

Using Jams, Jellies, Curds and Mincemeat.

Jam Tart Bonanza

These are great for childrens parties as they are colourful mini tarts much loved by children. It is also a good way of using up any last bits of preserves in a fun way.

Make this using sweet shortcrust pastry as it can be rolled very thinly and makes a crisp 'melt in the mouth' base.

For the pastry:

225g / 8oz plain flour
110g / 4oz firm butter, straight from the fridge
½ teaspoon salt
25g / 1oz golden caster sugar
2 egg yolks
1 tablespoon cold water

Home made jam and preserves of your choice

1. Sift the flour and salt together in a bowl and rub in the butter lightly, lifting up the mixture as you rub so as to keep the pastry airy and cool.

2. Stir in the sugar.

3. Beat the egg yolks with the cold water and stir into the dry ingredients with a knife.

4. Combine by hand to form a soft dough.

5. Roll out the pastry on a lightly floured surface and cut out rounds.

6. Grease some shallow bun or tart tins and place a round of pastry in each section. Press down lightly and put a teaspoon of various preserves in the centre of each tart. Try lemon curd and marmalade or any jam or jelly. The more and varied colours you combine, the better.

7. Bake for 12-15 minutes at 190C/Gas mark 5 until golden and crisp.

Don't overfill the tarts as they will bubble over and spoil the finished look. You could also get the children to fill them and then not have to worry too much about what they look like!

These will keep for a few days in an airtight container.

Queen of Puddings

180-200g / 6-8oz cake, broken into pieces
4 large eggs, separated
570ml / 1 pint milk
4-5 tablespoons of any home made jam,
marmalade or any other preserve
110g / 4oz caster sugar

1. Grease an oven proof dish and put the cake in the bottom.

2. Beat the egg yolks into the milk and pour over the cake. Press down and make sure the cake is well covered with the milk mixture.

3. Place in the oven at 180°C / Gas mark 4 for 30-35 minutes until the egg and milk mixture has set and the top is golden brown. Turn the oven down to 150°C / Gas mark 2.

4. Spread the preserve over the top of the hot base.

5. Whisk the egg whites until they are stiff and form peeks. Then fold in the sugar with a metal spoon.

6. Spread the meringue topping over the pudding and put in the oven for 20 minutes until the meringue is firm and golden. Serve immediately.

Paris Sandwich

350g / 12oz plain flour
225g / 8oz butter
125g / 4oz golden caster sugar
3 tablespoons home made raspberry jam

1. Rub the butter into the flour until the mixture looks like breadcrumbs and stir in the sugar.

2. Combine all the ingredients by hand to make a smooth dough.

3. Cut the mixture into 2 equal parts and press one half into the base of a buttered rectangular tin. Don't take the mixture up the sides, though.

4. Spread the jam over the shortbread base.

5. Using the other half of the shortbread, roll it out to form a rectangle the same size as the tin. Place it on top of the jam and prick the top with a fork.

6. Bake for 40 minutes at 180°C / gas mark 4.

7. When cooked, cut it into 12-14 fingers and dust with a little extra caster sugar.

This keeps for 4-5 days in an airtight tin.

Lemon Streusel Tray Bake

For the base:
120g / 4oz butter
60g / 2oz caster sugar
150g / 6oz plain flour
4-5 tablespoons home made lemon curd

For the topping:
150g / 6oz plain flour
½ teaspoon baking powder
120g / 4oz butter
85g / 3oz brown sugar
35g / 2½oz flaked almonds
Grated zest of a lemon

1. Cream the butter and sugar together until pale and fluffy.

2. Stir in the flour to make a soft dough. Press into a buttered rectangular tin and bake for 15 minutes at 180°C / gas mark 4. Remove it from the oven and allow to it cool for 5 minutes, then spread with the lemon curd.

4. For the topping, sieve the flour and baking powder together and rub in the butter. Stir in the sugar, almonds and lemon zest. Sprinkle the topping over the lemon curd and bake for 35 minutes at the same temperature as before.

5. Allow to cool and cut into 12-14 fingers

Black Forest Dessert Cake

For the sponges:

200g / 8oz self-raising flour
200g / 8oz golden caster sugar
200g / 8oz softened butter
3 eggs
2 level tablespoons cocoa powder
2 tablespoons milk
100g / 4oz dark chocolate, melted in a bowl
over a pan of hot water
4 tablespoons brandy or cherry liqueur

For the filling:

4-5 tablespoons home made black cherry
conserve
150ml / ¼ pint whipping cream, whisked until
firm
Grated dark chocolate for topping

1. Grease and line two 8 inch sandwich tins.

2. Cream the butter and sugar together in a mixing
bowl until soft and fluffy.

3. Beat in the eggs with a tablespoon of flour.
Then sieve together the cocoa powder and the
rest of the flour into a seperate bowl.

4. Stir in the melted chocolate and fold in the

Making Jams and Preserves

flour and cocoa mixture.

5. Divide the mixture evenly between the two tins and make a small well in the centre of the mixture to stop it rising too much in the middle.

6. Bake at 190°C / Gas mark 5 for 25 minutes until it is firm to the touch and springs back when pressed.

7. Leave it in the tin for 5 minutes to cool slightly before removing the paper. Place on a cooling rack and cool completely. Sprinkle over the brandy or cherry liqueur and leave it to soak into the sponge.

8. Sandwich the cakes together using the preserve and a little whipped cream.

9. Spread the cream over the top of the cake and sprinkle with grated chocolate.

Mincemeat and Apple Pie

225g / 8oz shortcrust pastry
½ jar of home made mincemeat
2 Bramley apples, peeled, cored, sliced and left
in water with a tablespoon of lemon juice (to
stop discolouration)
2 tablespoons caster sugar
A couple of knobs of butter

1. Grease a deep pie dish and line it with two thirds of the shortcrust pastry.

2. Spread the mincemeat over the bottom of the pie and arrange the apples over the top of the mincemeat.

3. Cover the pie with a pastry lid and bake at 200°C / Gas mark 6 for 30 minutes until the pastry is golden brown.

Blackcurrant Sorbet

6 tablespoons home made blackcurrant jelly
150g / 5oz caster sugar
575ml / 1 pint water
2 egg whites
4 tablespoons homemade blackcurrant syrup

1. Put all the ingredients, except for the egg white, into a pan over a low heat and stir gently until all the sugar has dissolved and the jelly has melted. Raise the heat and simmer for 5 minutes.

2. Allow it to cool, then put it into a large container and store in the freezer. When it is almost frozen, whisk the egg whites in a bowl until stiff and fold them into the iced mixture. Put it back in the freezer to freeze completely.

Serve in tall sorbet glasses with a little extra blackcurrant syrup.

Gooseberry Sponge Pudding

150g / 5oz self-raising flour
150g / 5oz soft brown sugar
150g / 5oz butter, softened
3 eggs, beaten
3 tablespoons gooseberry jam

1. Grease a 2 pint pudding basin or an ovenproof dish.

2. Put all the ingredients together in a mixing bowl and mix them together, preferably with a hand electric mixer. Continue mixing for 3-4 minutes until all the ingredients are thoroughly combined and the mixture is light and fluffy.

3. Put the jam in the base of the bowl or dish and spread it evenly.

4. Spread the cake mixture over the jam and make a small well in the top to keep the surface even.

5. Bake for 30-40 minutes at 190°C / Gas mark 5 until well risen and golden brown on the top.

Winter Conserve Roly Poly

225g / 8oz plain flour
110g / 4oz shredded vegetarian suet
½ teaspoon salt
2 level teaspoons baking powder
100ml / 4fl oz water
7-8 tablespoons home made winter conserve

1. Sieve the flour, salt and baking powder together in a bowl.

2. Stir in the suet and mix well.

3. Add the water and stir until combined. Bring the dough together by hand.

4. Roll the pastry out on a lightly floured surface until it measures about 20 x 30cm (8 by 12˝).

5. Spread the conserve over the pastry but don't take it right to the edge. Leave a small area around the pastry free so that it doesn't bubble out during cooking, although some will inevitably escape.

6. Roll the pudding up from the shortest edge, securing it down with a little water. Squeeze the ends together.

7. Place it on a greased baking tray and bake for 30-35 minutes at 200°C / Gas mark 6.

Glazes For Roast Meats

Most roast meats taste even better if they are given a glaze either before or during the cooking time. Homemade preserves are ideal for this and give a really delicious finish to the meat.

Poultry and Game

Glaze a roasting duck half way through the cooking time with orange marmalade or jelly if you don't like the peel. Use about 3 tablespoons spread evenly over the duck.

Spread 3-4 tablespoons of gooseberry jelly over a roasting goose to give it a tangy finish and an interesting flavour to the gravy.

Glaze chicken drumsticks with cranberry jelly and roast them for 30 minutes. These are good served hot or cold for a picnic.

Try putting chicken breasts in foil with a teaspoon of lemon jelly on the top. Seal the foil and bake in the oven for 30 minutes at 200°C / Gas mark 6.

Pork and Ham

Spread apple jelly over a leg or a shoulder joint of pork half way through the cooking time and serve a little extra with the cooked joint.

Making Jams and Preserves

When cooking pork steaks, glaze them with a little sage herb jelly before either grilling or frying.

Glaze a ham or a bacon joint with orange jelly about 30 minutes before the cooking time ends.

Beef and Lamb

Glaze a leg or a shoulder joint of lamb with red currant jelly about 40 minutes before the end of the cooking time.

When cooking a beef joint, glaze it with some blackberry jelly during the cooking. The flavour of the fruit with the beef is wonderful.

Lamb and Mint Kebabs

450g / 1lb minced lamb
1 level teaspoon salt
3 tablespoons home made mint jelly
1 tablespoon chopped fresh mint

1. Combine all the ingredients well in a bowl. Either make burger shaped rounds or squeeze some of the mixture round metal skewers.

2. Place the kebabs on an oiled baking tray and cook for 20 minutes at 200°C / Gas mark 6 until cooked through.

Using Pickles, Chutneys and Sauces

Pork and Pickle Pie

This is a tasty variation of the pork pie and goes well with salads or picnics.

For the pastry:

500g / 17oz plain flour
1 level teaspoon salt
500ml / 1 pint water
250g / 8½oz lard

1. Put the water in a pan and heat it to boiling. Add the lard and remove it from the heat. Stir the mixture until all the fat has melted into the water.

2. Sieve the flour and salt together in a mixing bowl.

3. Make a well in the flour and pour in the hot, lardy water and mix thoroughly to make a stiff dough.

For the filling:

800g / 2lb pork cut into fine cubes
2 teaspoons salt
¼ teaspoon black pepper
5-6 tablespoons home made brown pickle

Making Jams and Preserves

To make the pie:

1. Grease a 22cm / 9″ round tin, preferably one with a loose bottom.

2. Roll out two thirds of the pastry to line the tin and put half of the meat in the pastry case.

3. Spread the pickle over the pork and put the rest of the pork over the layer of pickle.

4. Roll out the pastry lid and put it on top of the pie. Dampen the edges so that the top sticks to the bottom and forms a seal. Crimp round the edge with a fork or using your finger and thumb. Glaze it with a little egg and milk mixture and make a hole or two in the centre of the pie to allow the steam to escape.

5. Bake at 180°C / Gas mark 4 for 1½ to 2 hours. Check that the meat is cooked in the centre of the pie by pushing a skewer through the middle of the; if anything other than a little pickle remains on the skewer then cook it for 10 more minutes and check again.

Beef in Wow Wow Sauce

450g / 1lb stewing beef, cubed
½ pint beef stock
100g / 4oz finely chopped mushrooms
5 chopped pickled walnuts
½ teaspoon dry mustard powder
3 tablespoons port
1 tablespoon freshly chopped parsley
1 tablespoon seasoned flour

1. Roll the meat in the seasoned flour and fry it gently in a little oil until it is just brown.

2. Put it into a casserole dish and sprinkle over the mustard powder and pour over the stock.

3. Put it into a pre-heated oven at 200°C / Gas mark 6 and cook for 30 minutes. Remove it from the oven and add the port and chopped mushrooms.

4. Turn down the heat to 180°C / Gas mark 4 and cook for 1¼ hours. Remove it from the oven and stir in the walnuts and parsley. Check and adjust the seasoning as necessary. Place it back in the oven for a further 30 minutes.

Serve with boiled potatoes and a green vegetable.

Beef and Tomato Relish Burgers

Mix 450g / 1lb of minced lean steak in a bowl and add two tablespoons of tomato relish and some salt and black pepper to taste. Combine them thoroughly by hand and shape small amounts into round patties using either a cutter or a baking ring as a guide to the size. Fry the burgers in a little oil and serve in a toasted bread bun.

Chicken and Corn Relish Burgers

Mix together the same quantities of meat and corn relish as in the previous recipe, but add a crushed clove of garlic with the seasoning. Prepare and fry the burgers in the same way as before.

For a tasty snack combine 100g / 4oz cheddar cheese with 1 tablespoon of home made mixed pepper chutney or tomato chutney and spread it on pieces of toast. Grill them for a few minutes until the cheese just begins to bubble.

Appendices

Making Jams and Preserves

Resources

Ascot Smallholding Supplies
www.ascott.biz
Everything for the smallholding and home farmer
including jam and cheese making equipment.
0845 1306285

Crocks and Pots
www.crocksandpots.co.uk
A wide range of professional catering equipment
for the domestic kitchen.
0208 144 5517

Lakeland Ltd.
www.lakeland.co.uk
Carrying a wide range of jam making equipment,
containers etc.
01539 488100

AlaCook - The Cook Shop
www.alacook.co.uk
A good range of jam making equipment as well
as other kitchen gadgets.
0800 0436199

Philip Morris & Son
www.philipmorris.uk.com
All sorts of jam making equipment, including
pans designed for Agas.
01432 377089

Oven Temperatures		
°C	°F	Gas
140	275	1
150	300	2
170	325	3
180	350	4
190	375	5
200	400	6
220	425	7
230	450	8
240	475	9
For fan-assisted ovens reduce the temperature by 20°C		

American Cup Conversions		
American	Imperial	Metric
1 cup flour	5oz	150 gm
1 cup sugar	8oz	225 gm
1 cup butter	8oz	225 gm
1 cup sultanas	7oz	200 gm

Making Jams and Preserves

Volume	
Imperial	Metric
2 fl oz	55 ml
3 fl oz	75 ml
5 fl oz (¼ pint)	150 ml
10 fl oz (½ pint)	570 ml
1¼ pint	725 ml
1¾ pint	1 litre
2 pint	1.2 litre
2½ pint	1.5 litre
4 pint	2.25 litre

By the same author

The Bread and Butter Book

Contents

Published by The Good Life Press Ltd.
ISBN 9 781 90487 134 7

The Good Life Press Ltd.
PO Box 536
Preston
PR2 9ZY
01772 652693

The Good Life Press Ltd. publishes a wide range of titles for the smallholder, farmer and country dweller as well as Home Farmer, the monthly magazine for anyone who wants to grab a slice of the good life - whether they live deep in the city or in the heart of the country.

Other titles of interest:

A Guide to Traditional Pig Keeping by Carol Harris
An Introduction to Keeping Sheep by J. Upton/D. Soden
Build It! by Joe Jacobs
Craft Cider Making by Andrew Lea
First Buy a Field by Rosamund Young
Flowerpot Farming by Jayne Neville
Grow and Cook by Brian Tucker
How to Butcher Livestock and Game by Paul Peacock
Precycle! by Paul Peacock
Talking Sheepdogs by Derek Scrimgeour
The Bread and Butter Book by Diana Sutton
The Cheese Making Book By Paul Peacock
The Pocket Guide to Wild Food by Paul Peacock
The Polytunnel Companion by Jayne Neville
The Sausage Book by Paul Peacock
Showing Sheep by Sue Kendrick
The Smoking and Curing Book by Paul Peacock
The Urban Farmer's Handbook by Paul Peacock
A Cut Above the Rest (A DVD guide to butchering)

www.goodlifepress.co.uk
www.homefarmer.co.uk
For more recipes visit www.precycle-it.co.uk